Black Lives Matter

Black Lives Matter

From a Moment to a Movement

Laurie Collier Hillstrom

An Imprint of ABC-CLIO, LLC

Santa Barbara, California • Denver, Colorado

Library of Congress Cataloging-in-Publication Data

Names: Hillstrom, Laurie Collier, 1965- author.
Title: Black Lives Matter : From a Moment to a Movement / Laurie
    Collier Hillstrom.
Description: Santa Barbara : Greenwood, 2018. | Includes bibliographical references and index. |
    Identifiers: LCCN 2018022898 (print) | LCCN 2018034688 (ebook) | ISBN
    9781440865718 (ebook) | ISBN 9781440865701 (hard copy : alk. paper)
Subjects: LCSH: Black lives matter movement—History. | African
    Americans—Social conditions—21st century. | African Americans—Civil
    rights—History—21st century. | Racial profiling in law
    enforcement—United States. | United States—Race relations.
Classification: LCC E185.615 (ebook) | LCC E185.615 .H518 2018 (print) | DDC
    323.1196073—dc23
LC record available at https://lccn.loc.gov/2018022898

ISBN: 978-1-4408-6570-1 (print)
       978-1-4408-6571-8 (eBook)

22 21 20 19 18   1 2 3 4 5

This book is also available as an eBook.

Greenwood
An Imprint of ABC-CLIO, LLC

ABC-CLIO, LLC
130 Cremona Drive, P.O. Box 1911
Santa Barbara, California 93116-1911
www.abc-clio.com

This book is printed on acid-free paper ∞

Manufactured in the United States of America

Contents

Introduction

#BlackLivesMatter started out as a hashtag on social media. It was originally created and shared by three black women—Alicia Garza, Patrisse Cullors, and Opal Tometi—who were longtime social justice activists and organizers. Garza inspired it by posting an anguished "Love Letter to Black People" on Facebook in 2012, after learning that a Florida jury had acquitted neighborhood watch volunteer George Zimmerman in the fatal shooting of 17-year-old Trayvon Martin. Anger and frustration over Martin's death and Zimmerman's acquittal led to grassroots organizing and protest actions in various cities across the country. "Many of us were tired and disturbed by the lack of recognition towards the killings of black people by vigilantes and law enforcement," Cullors recalled. "We were tired of it not leading the news. We were tired of it not being a part of the conversation around racial justice. We were like, 'What are we going to do next? What's the strategy?'"[1]

Concern about the issue of police violence against black people continued to simmer beneath the surface until 2014, when it exploded into the national consciousness following a spate of police-involved deaths of unarmed black men. Eric Garner died on July 17 after being restrained in an illegal choke hold by New York Police Department

(NYPD) officers. An eyewitness video recorded Garner saying "I can't breathe" over and over again while he was being pinned down on the sidewalk. Then, on August 9, 18-year-old Michael Brown was shot to death during an altercation with a white police officer, Darren Wilson, in Ferguson, Missouri. The sense of outrage over Brown's death was compounded by the fact that police investigators left Brown's body lying in the street in a puddle of blood for several hours. Bystanders subsequently posted images of the gruesome scene on social media. "It was a disrespected death," said Ferguson protester Kayla Reed. "It is repulsive that he had to lay there for four and a half hours and that his own grandmother had to plead that a sheet be put over his body."[2]

Tensions had been rising between Ferguson's black community and its primarily white police force for years. Brown's death ignited a firestorm of protest, from candlelight vigils, peaceful marches, and passionate speeches to broken windows, overturned cars, and flaming buildings. Ferguson police responded aggressively, employing armored vehicles, riot gear, rubber bullets, and tear gas against the protesters. Images of the unrest on the streets of Ferguson dominated the national news for weeks, garnering the attention of people across the country. The creators of the #BlackLivesMatter hashtag helped organize Freedom Rides that brought more than 500 activists from 18 different cities to Ferguson, where the various grassroots groups began to converge into a national campaign under the banner Black Lives Matter (BLM). "The NAACP didn't send their special-ops team," said DeRay Mckesson, who was inspired to drive nine hours from Minneapolis to join the protests. "The churches didn't organize in the way we thought they would. We had to figure it out."[3]

From a Moment to a Movement

For a movement that originated with a hashtag, it is little wonder that social media became a driving force in the growth of BLM. Activists on the ground during the Ferguson protests used platforms such as Twitter, Instagram, and Facebook to share observations, images, and videos that often challenged the official version of events presented in the mainstream media. Mckesson emerged as one of the most compelling voices documenting the confrontations between protesters and law enforcement in Ferguson, and he eventually reached more than 1 million followers on Twitter. Most importantly, the BLM activists connected the dots to assert that the fatal shooting of Brown was not an isolated incident but part of a pattern of police brutality, violence, and lack of accountability that grew out of systemic racism. In this way, they turned a moment into a movement. "The new movement is powerful yet diffuse, linked not by physical closeness or even necessarily by political consensus, but by the mobilizing force of social media," Elizabeth Day wrote in the *Guardian*. "A hashtag on Twitter can link the disparate fates of unarmed black men shot down by white police in a way that transcends geographical boundaries and time zones. A shared post on Facebook can organize a protest in a matter of minutes. Documentary photos and videos can be distributed on Tumblr pages and Periscope feeds. . . . Fatalities at the hands of police are now front-page news. They can no longer be ignored."[4]

BLM has its roots in the centuries-long black struggle for equality in America, and organizers have built upon the foundations laid by the civil rights and Black Power movements. From the beginning, however, BLM has emphasized diversity, inclusion, and empowerment in a way that the hierarchical, male-dominated movements of earlier eras did not. "We wanted to create a political space within and amongst our communities for activism that could stand firmly on the shoulders of movements that have come before us, such as the civil rights movement, while innovating on its strategies, practices and approaches to finally centralize the leadership of those existing at the margins of our economy and our society,"[5] explained Tometi, the daughter of Nigerian immigrants. Her two cofounders, Garza and Cullors, both identify as queer. They envisioned BLM as a "leaderful" movement that welcomed contributions and encouraged innovation by women, LGBTQ people, immigrants, low-income people, incarcerated people, young people, people with disabilities, and other frequently marginalized populations.

BLM developed as a decentralized, member-led network with around 40 local chapters in the United States, Canada, Australia, and Europe. The BLM network collaborates with dozens of affiliated organizations—such as the Black Youth Project 100, Dream Defenders, and Million Hoodies Movement for Justice—on protests and policy proposals through the Movement for Black Lives collective. BLM also encompasses countless individual donors, volunteers, protesters, and other supporters who devote their time, money, energy, or social media presence to the cause of ending police violence toward black people. "What unites the broad tent of BLM organizations and voices is a frustration with the lack of accountability for police who use excessive force, and with the state's typical response: a task force or commission report that garners laudatory headlines and leads nowhere," wrote Martha Biondi in *In These Times*. "Instead, this generation envisions more far-reaching change, including, even, a world without police. The insistent radicalism of the movement's demands and tactics place it at the vanguard of a reenergized Left."[6]

The forms of resistance employed by the individuals and groups aligned with the BLM movement have ranged from making phone calls, sharing information on social media, and holding meetings to blocking highways, disrupting political rallies, and organizing protest marches. BLM activists have staged die-in protests, in which hundreds of people lie on the ground as if they have been shot, at shopping malls and on college campuses. They have held up signs or unfurled banners at sporting events and concert venues. They have shouted down speakers, stormed the stage, or grabbed the microphone at campaign rallies and political conventions. They have blocked mass transit or shut down highways in Atlanta, Chicago, Dallas, Denver, Los Angeles, Minneapolis, Toronto, and other cities. Most protest actions target individuals or institutions that benefit from white privilege—systemic advantages that are often invisible to white people—in order to raise public awareness of racial bias and socioeconomic disparities. "This conversation has been happening between black people for centuries, and white people don't even have to acknowledge it exists," said BLM activist Mica Grim. "When we shut down the highway, it forces the conversation. It's also our way of showing Middle America a little piece of the inconvenience that it is to be a person of color every day."[7]

Controversy and Criticism

The BLM movement has generated controversy ever since the Ferguson protests, which at times could be characterized as riots.

Opponents of the movement have leveled various charges at BLM activists, claiming that they are disorganized, unfocused, unruly, radical, violent, antipolice, or antiwhite. Some older black leaders have expressed dismay at BLM's disruptive tactics, which often stand in contrast to the peaceful, dignified, respectable approach civil rights activists used in the past. "It is a large, free-wheeling movement without clear leaders, and individual participants have no doubt acted badly on many occasions," *Atlantic* writer Conor Friedersdorf said of BLM, "as is true of groups as varied as the Sons of Liberty in 1775, anti-Vietnam War protesters, and the Tea Party."[8]

Much public disapproval has centered around the organization's name, Black Lives Matter. Some critics have described it as inherently racist because they think it implies that only black lives matter, or that black lives matter more than other lives. Detractors have suggested the alternative terms "All Lives Matter" and "Blue Lives Matter" to emphasize the equal value of white people's lives and police officers' lives. The BLM movement's founders reject this point of view, however. They insist that explicitly affirming the value of black lives does not diminish the value of other lives. They also contend that protecting black lives is a necessary step toward achieving the goal of making all lives matter.

The BLM movement has come under increased public scrutiny since July 2016, when eight police officers were killed in ambush-style attacks in Dallas, Texas, and Baton Rouge, Louisiana. Although the gunmen were not formally associated with BLM—and leaders of the movement condemned their actions—commentators on the political right claimed that BLM's antipolice rhetoric and protests had created a hostile atmosphere that imperiled the lives of law enforcement officers. The movement has faced additional challenges under the administration of President Donald Trump, who has expressed antipathy toward BLM protesters. In August 2017, for instance, Trump assigned "blame on both sides"[9] following a violent clash between white supremacists and counter-protesters from BLM and other progressive groups in Charlottesville, Virginia. As part of an increasingly virulent "alt-right" backlash against the movement, some opponents have even falsely tried to portray BLM as a hate group or a domestic terrorist organization composed of "black identity extremists."

Significance and Impact

Leaders of the BLM movement view the backlash as evidence that their strategies have been effective in challenging white privilege and raising awareness of racial inequality. The movement has made important gains in its few years of existence, such as compiling statistics on police violence, prompting federal investigations of police practices, and proposing a slate of policies for criminal justice reform. "Black Lives Matter's name and racial justice message are now ubiquitous," Emily Parker wrote in *Medium*. "Black Lives Matter has coincided with the longest, sustained, national attention to racial issues since the early 1970s, when race fell off the list of Americans' most important issues facing the country."[10]

As the BLM movement has matured, it has broadened its focus to include what it describes as institutionalized racism in the United States. BLM activists have increasingly fought for comprehensive measures to dismantle barriers to advancement for black people and create equal opportunities in education, employment, housing, and income. "The question isn't about that moment [when a black citizen is confronted by a police officer]," Cullors noted. "If we sort of rewind time, what resources did they have in that neighborhood? Do they have access to after-school programming? Do they have access to career development? I'm talking about really basic things that can lead to different life choices for black people, that can lead to a different experience and a different interaction with law enforcement."[11]

BLM has also joined forces with progressive groups that have formed since the 2016 election to work to reform immigration policies, increase the minimum wage, adopt stricter gun-control laws, and pursue other issues of concern to black communities. Many of these new movements have employed strategies and tactics pioneered by BLM. Biondi credited BLM with "reminding us of the power of mass action, moral outrage, youth leadership, civil disobedience, boisterous demonstrations, sophisticated use of media and spirited ideological debate in building a left consciousness and a movement."[12] BLM received international recognition in November 2017, when the movement's founders were awarded the Sydney Peace Prize in Australia. "Black Lives Matter has become what black communities all over the world have needed it to become. At times it is a hashtag, at other moments it is a declaration, a cry of rage, a sharing of light. It has become a movement that is international, worldwide in its scope of liberation for black and oppressed people everywhere," Cullors declared in her acceptance speech. "BLM is a growing global movement."[13]

Notes

1. Touré, "A Year Inside the Black Lives Matter Movement," *Rolling Stone*, December 7, 2017, https://www.rollingstone.com/politics/news/toure-inside -black-lives-matter-w513190.
2. Ibid.
3. Ibid.
4. Elizabeth Day, "#BlackLivesMatter: The Birth of a New Civil Rights Movement," *Guardian*, July 19, 2015, https://www.theguardian.com/world/ 2015/jul/19/blacklivesmatter-birth-civil-rights-movement.
5. Opal Tometi, "Celebrating MLK Day: Reclaiming Our Movement Legacy," *Huffington Post*, January 18, 2015, https://www.huffingtonpost.com/opal-tometi/ reclaiming-our-movement-l_b_6498400.html.
6. Martha Biondi, "The Radicalism of Black Lives Matter," *In These Times*, August 15, 2016, http://inthesetimes.com/features/black-lives-matter-history -police-brutality.html.
7. Touré, "A Year Inside the Black Lives Matter Movement."
8. Conor Friedersdorf, "How to Distinguish between Antifa, White Suprema-cists, and Black Lives Matter," *Atlantic*, August 31, 2017, https://www .theatlantic.com/politics/archive/2017/08/drawing-distinctions-antifa-the-alt -right-and-black-lives-matter/538320/.
9. Andrew Rafferty, Marianna Sotomayor, and Daniel Arkin, "Trump Says 'Two Sides' Share Blame for Charlottesville Rally Violence," NBC News, August 16, 2017, https://www.nbcnews.com/news/us-news/trump-defends -all-sides-comment-n793001.
10. Emily Parker and Charlton McIlwain, "#BlackLivesMatter and the Power and Limits of Social Media," *Medium*, December 2, 2016, https://medium.com/ @emilydparker/how-blacklivesmatter-resembles-activism-in-the-authoritarian -world-24d1200864f6.
11. Touré, "A Year Inside the Black Lives Matter Movement."
12. Biondi, "The Radicalism of Black Lives Matter."
13. Patrisse Cullors, "Speech for the Sydney Peace Prize," November 6, 2017, http://patrissecullors.com/2017/11/06/speech-sydney-peace-prize/.

Timeline

1896   The U.S. Supreme Court's controversial decision in *Plessy v. Ferguson* permits the segregation of public facilities by race, as long as the accommodations provided to black and white citizens are "separate but equal."

1954   In a major legal victory for the civil rights movement, the Supreme Court overturns *Plessy* with its landmark ruling in *Brown v. Board of Education*, which declares segregated schools to be "inherently unequal" and a violation of black citizens' rights under the Fourteenth Amendment to the U.S. Constitution.

1955   August 28—The lynching of 14-year-old Emmett Till in Mississippi for allegedly flirting with a white woman helps generate public support for the civil rights movement.

December 1—Civil rights activist Rosa Parks is arrested in Montgomery, Alabama, for violating the city bus system's segregated seating policy, sparking a yearlong bus boycott by black residents.

1956   The Montgomery Bus Boycott culminates in *Browder v. Gayle*, a Supreme Court ruling that finds racial segregation of public transit unconstitutional.

1957 Segregationists prevent nine black students from integrating Central High School in Little Rock, Arkansas.

1960 February 1—Four black college students challenge the segregation of public facilities by staging a sit-in protest at Woolworth's lunch counter in Greensboro, North Carolina.

December 5—In *Boynton v. Virginia*, the Supreme Court rules that segregation of interstate transportation facilities—such as waiting areas, ticket counters, and restrooms—violates the Interstate Commerce Act.

1961 Groups of black and white activists with the Congress of Racial Equality (CORE) embark on a series of integrated bus trips known as Freedom Rides to test compliance with federal desegregation orders in various cities.

1963 April—Martin Luther King Jr. and other civil rights leaders launch a campaign of mass protests against segregation in Birmingham, Alabama.

June 11—Alabama Governor George Wallace stands in the doorway of a building on the University of Alabama campus to block two black students from entering.

August 28—An estimated 250,000 people participate in the March on Washington for Jobs and Freedom, where King delivers his famous "I Have a Dream" speech.

1964 March 7—Civil rights activists involved in the Selma-Montgomery Voting Rights March are attacked and beaten by Alabama law enforcement as they attempt to cross the Edmund Pettus Bridge.

July 2—The Civil Rights Act of 1964 becomes law, formally ending legal segregation in the United States.

1965 August 6—The Voting Rights Act of 1965 prohibits racial discrimination in voting requirements and establishes federal oversight of jurisdictions that used such measures to suppress minority voting rights.

August 11–16—Violent riots occur in the predominantly black Watts neighborhood of Los Angeles, leaving 34 people dead and causing $40 million in property damage.

1966   July 28—Stokely Carmichael, leader of the Student Nonviolent Coordinating Committee (SNCC), launches the Black Power movement at a rally in Mississippi.

October 15—The militant Black Panther Party is founded by activists Huey P. Newton and Bobby Seale.

1967   Violent riots in the city of Detroit result in the deaths of 43 people and the destruction of nearly 1,400 buildings.

1968   February 29—The National Advisory Commission on Civil Disorders, commonly known as the Kerner Commission, releases a report attributing urban riots and civil unrest to persistent racial inequality.

April 4—King is assassinated in Memphis, Tennessee.

October 16—A notable Black Power demonstration occurs at the Olympic Games, when two African American track medalists raise black-gloved fists on the podium during the playing of the national anthem.

1991   January 15—The U.S. Supreme Court rules in *Oklahoma City v. Dowell* that school districts can be released from court-ordered integration plans once they demonstrate earnest compliance, even if it results in future segregation.

March 3—The videotaped beating of black motorist Rodney King by white police officers in Los Angeles raises awareness of the issue of police brutality toward African Americans.

2005   Florida passes a controversial "stand-your-ground" law that allows citizens to use deadly force in self-defense.

2008   Many Americans view the historic election of Barack Obama as the nation's first black president as the start of a promising new era in race relations.

2012   February 26—Trayvon Martin, an unarmed black teenager, is fatally shot during an altercation with neighborhood watch volunteer George Zimmerman in Sanford, Florida.

March 21—Around 1,000 people—most of them wearing hooded sweatshirts—attend the Million Hoodie March in New York City to protest Martin's death.

March 22—Twenty-two-year-old Rekia Boyd is shot and killed by an off-duty Chicago police officer after he confronts her group of friends in a city park.

March 22—A Change.org online petition calling for Zimmerman's arrest receives 1.3 million signatures.

March 23—President Obama calls for a full investigation of the Martin shooting.

April 11—Under intense public pressure and federal scrutiny, the Sanford Police Department finally arrests Zimmerman.

July 13—Zimmerman is found not guilty of second-degree murder under Florida's controversial stand-your-ground law.

July 13—Activist Alicia Garza responds to Zimmerman's acquittal by posting a heartfelt "Love Letter to Black People" on Facebook.

July 14—Inspired by Garza's message, activist Patrisse Cullors turns her friend's sentiments into a hashtag #BlackLivesMatter and shares the post.

July 15—Activist Opal Tometi creates a social media platform around the hashtag and encourages people to share their views about why black lives matter.

2013   In *Shelby County v. Holder*, the Supreme Court invalidates the preclearance provision of the Voting Rights Act of 1965, which had required jurisdictions with a history of discrimination against minority voters to obtain federal approval before changing their voting rules.

2014   February 16—Forty-seven-year-old Yvette Smith is shot and killed by a Texas deputy when she answers the door after calling 911 to report a domestic disturbance.

July 17—Eric Garner dies after being restrained in a choke hold by New York Police Department (NYPD) officers and repeatedly saying "I can't breathe."

August 5—Twenty-two-year-old John Crawford is shot to death by police after picking up a toy gun while shopping at a Walmart store in Ohio.

August 9—Eighteen-year-old Michael Brown is shot and killed by Officer Darren Wilson in Ferguson, Missouri.

August 10–25—The city of Ferguson is the site of peaceful protests, violent riots, and militarized police responses following Brown's death.

August 13—National news footage shows Ferguson police firing tear gas at protesters.

August 15—Ferguson police identify Wilson as the officer involved in Brown's shooting and also release a surveillance video from a nearby convenience store depicting Brown's activities before he was killed.

August 18—National Guard troops arrive in Ferguson to help control the unrest.

August 20—St. Louis County Prosecuting Attorney Robert McCulloch convenes a grand jury to decide whether Wilson should be charged with a crime.

August 23—More than 2,500 people march on Staten Island to protest Garner's death.

Late August—More than 500 activists from 18 different cities participate in the Black Lives Matter (BLM) Freedom Ride to Ferguson.

October—Activists from BLM and other groups organize a series of Ferguson protest actions that include unfurling a banner at a St. Louis Symphony concert, disrupting a St. Louis Rams football game, and staging an overnight occupation of St. Louis University.

October 21—Missouri Governor Jay Nixon creates the Ferguson Commission to investigate police practices and make recommendations for reform.

November 13—Tanisha Anderson, a 37-year-old mother with bipolar disorder, dies after being forcibly restrained by Cleveland police officers responding to her family's request for help dealing with a manic episode.

November 22—Twelve-year-old Tamir Rice is fatally shot by a Cleveland police officer while playing with a pellet gun in a park near his home.

November 24—Demonstrations take place in 170 cities nationwide to protest the grand jury's decision not to indict Wilson.

November 28—BLM protesters disrupt busy holiday-season shopping at malls across the country by lying down on the floor as if they had been shot.

December 3—A Staten Island grand jury declines to indict an NYPD officer involved in Garner's death.

December 3—The U.S. Department of Justice (DOJ) launches an investigation into Garner's death.

December 8—LeBron James and other NBA players wear "I Can't Breathe" shirts to protest Garner's death.

December 20—A man shoots and kills two NYPD officers as they sit in a patrol car; his social media posts indicate that he viewed his actions as retribution for Garner.

2015   January 8—*Essence* magazine devotes an entire issue to the BLM movement.

March 4—A DOJ investigation reveals a pattern of civil rights violations by Ferguson law enforcement and court officials toward the city's black residents.

March—Activists DeRay Mckesson, Brittany Packnett, and Samuel Sinyangwe launch the Mapping Police Violence project, an interactive map of all police-involved deaths in cities across the United States.

April 4—Walter Scott runs away from a traffic stop in North Charleston, South Carolina, and is shot in the back by a white police officer.

April 12—Twenty-five-year-old Freddie Gray sustains fatal spinal injuries while in police custody in Baltimore.

April 19—Massive protests erupt in Baltimore following the death of Gray.

May 18—President Obama's Task Force on Twenty-First Century Policing issues recommendations for improving the relationship between municipal police departments and the local communities they serve.

May 20—The African American Policy Forum (AAPF) launches the #SayHerName campaign to raise awareness of black women victims of police violence.

June 17—A white supremacist gunman kills nine black church leaders in Charleston, South Carolina.

June 26—When BLM activist DeRay Mckesson attends a memorial service for victims of the Charleston church shootings, he becomes the focus of an angry Twitter campaign with the hashtag #GoHomeDeRay.

June 30—The video for Kendrick Lamar's song "Alright"—widely considered to be an anthem of the BLM movement—depicts the rapper being shot by police.

July 13—Social justice advocate Sandra Bland is found dead in her jail cell in Waller County, Texas, three days after being pulled over by a state trooper for failing to signal a lane change.

July 24—More than 2,000 activists gather at Cleveland State University and form the Movement for Black Lives, a coalition of groups involved in the BLM movement.

August 21—Mckesson, Packnett, and Sinyangwe launch Campaign Zero, a slate of proposed policy actions for state and local governments to take toward eliminating police violence.

2016   January—The hashtag #BlackLivesMatter has appeared on Twitter nearly 12 million times, making it one of the most popular social issues ever discussed on the platform.

February 7—Singer Beyoncé and her backup dancers wear costumes inspired by the Black Power movement during the Super Bowl halftime show.

February 24—BLM activists disrupt a campaign appearance by Democratic presidential candidate Hillary Clinton.

May—Louisiana becomes the first state to adopt a "Blue Lives Matter" bill that defines attacks on law enforcement officers as hate crimes.

July 6—Alton Sterling is shot five times in the chest while he is being restrained on the ground by Baton Rouge police officers.

July 7—Philando Castile is shot and killed by a police officer during a routine traffic stop in St. Paul, Minnesota; his girlfriend live-streams the fatal encounter on Facebook.

July 7—A sniper kills five police officers during a BLM protest in Dallas; the shooter says his motive was retaliation for recent shootings of black men by white police officers.

July 8—The Dallas police shootings engender a negative shift in public opinion about the BLM movement.

July 17—A gunman described as a "black separatist" kills three police officers and injures three others in a purported revenge shooting in Baton Rouge.

July 18–21—At the Republican National Convention, Milwaukee County Sheriff David A. Clarke and other speakers express support for law enforcement and claim that BLM protests inflame racial tensions and generate antipolice sentiment.

August 1—The Movement for Black Lives releases a political platform aimed at achieving the liberation of black communities in the United States.

August 10—A DOJ investigation stemming from the death of Freddie Gray reveals a pattern of racially biased police practices in Baltimore.

August 26—NFL quarterback Colin Kaepernick remains seated during the national anthem as a form of protest against police violence.

2017   January 20—Donald Trump is sworn into office as the 45th president of the United States.

January 21—The White House website is updated to include a statement expressing the administration's support for law enforcement and disapproval of BLM protesters.

January 27—BLM cofounders Garza, Cullors, and Tometi release a statement reemphasizing their commitment to the cause and describing Trump as a "white supremacist."

February—Attorney General Jeff Sessions announces his intention to discontinue federal oversight of city police departments with a history of racially biased practices.

August 3—The Federal Bureau of Investigation (FBI) releases an intelligence assessment entitled "Black Identity Extremists Likely Motivated to Target Law Enforcement Officers."

August 12—Hundreds of white nationalists, Ku Klux Klan (KKK) members, and neo-Nazis gather for a Unite the Right rally to protest the removal of a statue of Confederate General Robert E. Lee from a city park in Charlottesville, Virginia.

August 12—A deadly clash occurs in Charlottesville between white nationalists and counter-protesters from BLM and other progressive groups.

August 15—Trump defends the white supremacist protesters by claiming that there were "very fine people on both sides" of the conflict in Charlottesville.

August 28—Trump signs an executive order allowing local police departments to purchase surplus military equipment, reversing a ban that had been issued by the Obama administration after the Ferguson protests.

2018   A Mapping Police Violence report for 2017 indicates that 27 percent of the 1,147 people killed by police officers in the United States that year were African Americans.

CHAPTER ONE | Historical Roots of the Movement

Black people have struggled to gain equal rights and achieve social justice in America for centuries, ever since the first enslaved Africans were forcibly transported to the New World in the 1600s. The long history of black struggle includes such seminal phases as the abolitionist movement, the Underground Railroad, the resistance to segregation during the Jim Crow era, the nonviolent protests of the civil rights movement, the militancy of the Black Power movement, and the political expression of hip-hop culture. Supporters place the Black Lives Matter (BLM) movement within the context of these unfinished earlier movements to end racial discrimination and achieve equality. "Having once hoped that the election of the first black president meant that the tide of race relations in America might begin to turn, many young black Americans were forced to face the reality— by one high-profile police shooting after another—that living in a world in which they're treated like their white contemporaries remains an impossibility," Nathalie Baptiste wrote in the *Nation* in 2017. "But while Black Lives Matter arose in a moment of disappointment and grief, it has for the past four years also helped to inaugurate a new era in the struggle for racial justice."[1]

The Civil Rights Movement

BLM traces its roots to the civil rights movement, the decades-long fight to end racial segregation and discrimination in the United States. Although activists from the two eras have employed different strategies and tools, they share the goal of making the nation live up to its founding principles of equality and justice for all citizens. The civil rights movement began in the years following World War II. The 125,000 African Americans who fought overseas in segregated military units—as well as the millions of black workers who contributed to the war effort by producing tanks, planes, weapons, and supplies for the Allied forces—were less willing to accept second-class citizenship once the conflict ended. Many, like professional baseball pioneer Jackie Robinson, assumed active roles in the fight to improve the treatment of black people in American society.

An early battle in the fight to end racial segregation focused on the nation's public school system. Activists with the National Association for the Advancement of Colored People (NAACP) and other organizations viewed access to high-quality education as a key element in securing equal opportunity for African Americans. Since the U.S. Supreme Court's notorious 1896 decision in *Plessy v. Ferguson* had permitted public facilities to be segregated by race, however, most black students received an inferior education in poorly funded "colored" schools, which usually had run-down buildings, over-crowded classrooms, underpaid teachers, and outdated textbooks.

The NAACP challenged this situation by launching a series of lawsuits that were eventually consolidated as *Brown v. Board of Education*. The lead case involved an eight-year-old black girl from Topeka, Kansas, who was denied admission to the all-white school in her neighborhood by the city's board of education. This decision meant that she had to walk a mile and cut through a busy railroad yard to reach the bus stop for a distant colored school. NAACP attorney Thurgood Marshall presented the case to the Supreme Court, where he argued that segregation was harmful to black students and made them feel inferior. In its landmark 1954 decision, the Supreme Court declared segregated schools to be "inherently unequal" in violation of black citizens' right to equal protection of the law under the Fourteenth Amendment to the Constitution. Although many states and school districts found ways to delay, resist, or avoid complying with the ruling, it launched a series of efforts to end segregation in other areas of American life.

A year after the *Brown v. Board* ruling, civil rights activist Rosa Parks was arrested in Montgomery, Alabama, for violating the city bus system's segregated seating policy by refusing to relinquish her seat to a white passenger. The Montgomery Improvement Association, led by a young minister named Martin Luther King Jr., organized a year-long bus boycott by Montgomery's black residents, who had previously comprised 80 percent of riders. People carpooled, shared taxis, arranged shuttles, walked, or rode bicycles to avoid traveling by bus. By the time the Supreme Court ruled segregation of public transit unconstitutional in 1956 in *Browder v. Gayle*, the boycott had caused so much economic hardship for the bus company that the city immediately integrated its bus system.

Segregation of interstate bus travel was deemed illegal in 1946, and in 1960, the Supreme Court expanded its earlier ruling to require integration of waiting areas, ticket counters, restrooms, and other public facilities in bus terminals. Yet many states openly defied the order, especially in the South, and maintained strict segregation policies. In 1961, groups of black and white activists with the Congress of Racial Equality (CORE) embarked on a series of integrated bus trips known as Freedom Rides to test compliance in various cities. They encountered violent resistance from white segregationists at several points in their journeys. When a bus carrying Freedom Riders broke down outside of Anniston, Alabama, for instance, an angry mob descended on it, broke windows, and threw a firebomb inside. All of the Freedom Riders escaped unharmed, and an undercover state police officer prevented them from being attacked by the mob. News photographs of the burning bus shocked people across the country and increased public support for the civil rights movement.

Jim Crow laws in the South also segregated people by race in public spaces, such as hotels, restaurants, theaters, parks, and swimming pools. In 1960, four black college students mounted a challenge to these laws by requesting service at segregated lunch counter at a Woolworth's store in Greensboro, North Carolina. After being denied service, they remained in their seats and refused to leave, even when angry white segregationists shouted at, spit on, or punched them.

Their sit-in protest attracted national media attention and inspired similar direct actions in college towns across the South. Supporters in the North launched boycotts of Woolworth's and other national chains that practiced segregation, and the negative publicity eventually forced businesses to integrate.

Some of the most memorable protests of the civil rights movement took place in 1963 in Birmingham, Alabama. King and other leaders of the Southern Christian Leadership Conference (SCLC) chose Birmingham as the focal point of their campaign because the city's police force, led by Chief Eugene "Bull" Connor, had a history of violently suppressing desegregation efforts. As peaceful protesters marched through the streets, they were confronted by police in riot gear, snarling police dogs, tear gas, and high-pressure water hoses. Shocking scenes of police brutality appeared on television and in newspapers across the country. Later that year, civil rights leaders organized the March on Washington for Jobs and Freedom, which brought 250,000 people to the nation's capital to demand new federal legislation prohibiting racial discrimination in employment, housing, transportation, and education. These efforts eventually led to the passage of the Civil Rights Act of 1964, which formally ended legal segregation in the United States.

The final chapter in the civil rights movement was the campaign to secure black voting rights. Civil rights leaders understood that securing the right to vote would give African Americans an equal voice in the political system, which was key to creating meaningful and lasting change. Yet many states imposed voter-qualification rules that unfairly discriminated against black citizens, including poll taxes, literacy tests, and property ownership requirements. In their determination to maintain political control, white segregationists often used intimidation and violence to prevent black people from registering to vote. To draw attention to this situation, civil rights activists organized the Selma-Montgomery Voting Rights March in 1964. As 600 peaceful protesters left the Alabama town of Selma on their way to the state capital, they were attacked and beaten by 150 state and local law enforcement officers on the Edmund Pettus Bridge. More than 50 marchers were hospitalized for their injuries. The brutal confrontation helped generate support for passage of the Voting Rights Act of 1965, which prohibited the use of racially motivated voting

requirements and provided for federal oversight of elections in jurisdictions with a history of using such measures to suppress minority
voting rights.

Modern Parallels

Historians have pointed out many parallels between the civil
rights movement and the BLM movement. The death of a black
teenager—and graphic images that brought its brutal reality to national
attention—served as a major impetus for both movements. The lynching
of 14-year-old Emmett Till in 1955 for allegedly flirting with a white
woman in Mississippi, and his mother's insistence on an open casket to
display his battered body, generated public outrage that fueled later protests. Nearly 60 years later, the fatal shooting of 18-year-old Michael
Brown by a white police officer in Ferguson, Missouri, and images of
his body lying in the street that circulated on social media, sparked the
BLM movement. Other similarities between the two movements include
their youthful leadership, their use of media tools to gain support for
their message, and their reliance on such protest tactics as boycotts, sit-
ins, marches, and blocking traffic. "Whether it's segregated lunch counters or voting rights or whether it's police violence," said former Student
Nonviolent Coordinating Committee (SNCC) field secretary Charles
Cobb, "that's what protest does, it challenges with varying degrees of
intensity the status quo."[2]

Critics of BLM often compare it unfavorably to the earlier movement. Looking back, King and other civil rights leaders of the past are
considered American heroes who fought for a just cause. They are
remembered and revered six decades later as respectable, articulate,
and nonviolent. In contrast, BLM activists have been denounced as
disrespectful, disruptive, and violent. Yet historians note that public
perceptions of the civil rights movement were largely negative in the
1960s, and that many events considered admirable today were viewed
as unproductive, harmful, or radical at that time. A Gallup poll taken
in 1961, for instance, found that 61 percent of Americans disapproved
of the Freedom Rides, while 57 percent felt that sit-in protests hurt
rather than helped the cause of integration. Similarly, a poll taken in
1963 showed that 60 percent of Americans held an unfavorable view

of the March on Washington, which has been forever etched in history as the site of King's famous "I Have a Dream" speech.[3]

Khalil Gibran Muhammad, director of the Schomburg Center for Research in Black Culture at the New York Public Library, argued that the BLM movement represents a natural evolution of the civil rights movement. "There's a lot of similarity in recognizing that there are huge disparities that exist in this nation, and bringing attention to those disparities in ways that are about visibility for the suffering of the others and something that Dr. King called a confrontation with strength and dignity," he said. "The young people of the Black Lives Matter movement are doing the same, except their audience is a national audience through social media as well as the local organizing that goes on. But I will add this. They are fundamentally committed to moving past what they call respectability politics. They want to suggest that the work of transforming America now means that everyone is entitled to their human dignity and their due process. And if they don't speak perfect English, if they've not graduated from high school, they still deserve respect in this nation."[4]

The Black Power Movement

Some observers contend that BLM has more in common with the Black Power movement. By the mid-1960s, some civil rights activists grew disillusioned with the strategy of nonviolent resistance and argued that more aggressive tactics were needed to push the pace of social change. "The mounting militancy of the later 1960s didn't come out of nowhere," historian Jeanne Theoharis wrote in *A More Beautiful and Terrible History: The Uses and Misuses of Civil Rights History*. "It came from ignoring, denigrating, and rejecting the demands community organizers had made for years for real school desegregation and educational equity, open and affordable housing, jobs and a robust social safety net, equitable municipal services, and the transformation of the criminal justice system."[5]

Stokely Carmichael, leader of the SNCC, first popularized the term "black power" at a 1966 rally in Mississippi, where he gave a speech expressing the frustration and resentment felt by many black activists at that time. Some claimed that ending segregation was an insufficient goal, because being allowed to sit with white patrons in a restaurant was meaningless if black patrons lacked sufficient funds to pay for a meal. Others argued that legislation was not an effective cure for racism. They sought ways to address underlying, systemic sources of racial oppression, such as economic and political inequality.

The Black Power movement that rose to prominence in the late 1960s and early 1970s emphasized racial unity, pride, identity, and self-respect. Like BLM activists, Black Power supporters tended to be young, urban, and working class, in contrast to the older and more educated leaders of the main branch of the civil rights movement. Black Power activists adopted a raised fist as a symbol of their determination to organize and defend black interests and values. One of the most notable Black Power demonstrations occurred at the 1968 Summer Olympic Games, when two African American track medalists raised black-gloved fists on the podium during the playing of the national anthem. Black Power activists worked to strengthen black communities and make them self-sufficient by establishing black-owned businesses and social institutions. The Black Power movement also influenced American culture, from the introduction of the slogan "black is beautiful" to the establishment of Black Studies as an academic discipline at U.S. colleges.

Some of the organizations associated with the Black Power movement asserted that white power structures had to be destroyed through collective action in order for black people to achieve freedom and equality. Some activists advocated a complete withdrawal from mainstream American society, claiming that separatism and black nationalism were the only legitimate responses to racial discrimination and oppression. The Black Panther Party, a revolutionary socialist group founded by activists Huey P. Newton and Bobby Seale, represented the most aggressive and radical wing of the movement. Members wore uniforms consisting of black berets, black leather jackets, and dark sunglasses and carried firearms to symbolize black empowerment, militancy, and self-defense. Party leaders released a 10-point list of demands that included many of the same concerns later expressed by BLM activists, including racial equality in employment, housing, and education, and an end to police brutality and mass incarceration of African Americans.

Like the BLM movement, the Black Power movement forcefully challenged the status quo and generated opposition, fear, and hostility in many quarters. Critics portrayed it as violent, antiwhite, and anti-law enforcement, and federal authorities went to great lengths to discredit and criminalize it. "The movement was really considered an angry movement that practiced politics without portfolio and really is remembered by the images of gun-toting black urban militants, most notably the Black Panther Party," said historian Peniel Joseph. "I think that a lot of people think of the movement as being fundamentally unproductive, just kind of reinforcing white fears, for example, about black advancement, reinforcing racial segregation by pushing both blacks and whites into their corner."[6]

Police Brutality Sparks Urban Riots

The BLM demonstrations that erupted in Ferguson, Baltimore, Cleveland, New York, and other cities to protest the police-involved deaths of unarmed black citizens can be viewed as the latest in a long series of urban uprisings sparked by incidents of police brutality. "Since 1935, nearly every so-called race riot in the United States—and there have been more than 100—has been sparked by a police incident," wrote Nikole Hannah-Jones of ProPublica. "This can be an act of brutality, or a senseless killing. But the underlying causes run much deeper. Police, because they interact in black communities every day, are often seen as the face of larger systems of inequality in the justice system, employment, education, and housing."[7]

One of the precursors to the BLM protests occurred in the predominantly black Watts neighborhood of South Central Los Angeles in 1965. Two white policemen pulled over a 21-year-old black motorist for reckless driving, and a crowd gathered on the street as they gave the suspect a field sobriety test, which he failed. As the police prepared to arrest the man, a shouting match and scuffle ensued, during which one officer struck the suspect in the head with his baton. The crowd of spectators grew angry at what they viewed as racially motivated abuse by the police, and some people began throwing rocks and breaking windows.

Racial tensions had been rising in Los Angeles for some time. The Watts neighborhood had been mired in unemployment, poverty, and crime for years, and residents felt politically powerless following the repeal of a measure intended to protect minorities from housing discrimination. Against this background of simmering resentment and hostility, the traffic stop ignited five days of violent riots, with rampant looting, arson, beatings, and sniper fire at police and firefighters responding to the unrest. By the time National Guard troops managed to restore order, the violence had left 34 people dead and more than 1,000 injured, affected 50 square miles, and destroyed $40 million worth of property.

Two years later, the most destructive riots in U.S. history rocked the city of Detroit. The decline of the American automotive industry had led to "white flight" from the inner city to the surrounding suburbs. The city's black residents were left behind to grapple with a slate of urban problems that were aggravated by a decreasing tax base. Once-vital neighborhoods fell into disrepair, with poorly maintained infrastructure, vacant storefronts, and abandoned houses. In low-income, predominantly black neighborhoods, these problems were compounded by racial tensions between residents and the city's mostly white police force. Some residents viewed the Detroit Police as an occupying army that harassed and intimidated them, rather than protecting and serving them.

A police raid on an after-hours nightclub in the Virginia Park neighborhood was the precipitating incident of the 1967 Detroit Riots. As the vice squad waited for vehicles to transport patrons to the police station, a crowd gathered in the street and began throwing bottles. When one smashed the window of a police car, the remaining officers left the scene. Before long, hundreds of people were rampaging through the streets, smashing windows, looting businesses, setting fires, and attacking police and firefighters who responded to the unrest. By the time 7,000 National Guard and U.S. Army troops arrived to put down the riots, nearly 1,400 buildings had been burned, 43 people had been killed, and nearly 350 others had been injured.

Dozens of other riots or major incidents of civil disorder occurred in U.S. cities in the 1960s. President Lyndon B. Johnson responded by convening the National Advisory Commission on Civil Disorders, commonly known as the Kerner Commission, to investigate the causes of the unrest. In a scathing report released in 1968, the commission members placed the blame squarely on systemic racism and failed policies that kept black citizens segregated in substandard housing and offered them limited economic opportunities. "Our nation is moving toward two societies—one black and one white—separate and unequal," it concluded. "Discrimination and segregation have long permeated much of American life; they now threaten the future of every American."[8]

Few of the Kerner Commission's recommendations were implemented, however, and conditions failed to improve for black residents of many large cities throughout the 1970s and 1980s. Although riots occurred in Chicago, New York, Miami, and elsewhere during this period, the nation's attention largely turned to other issues, such as the Vietnam War, the women's liberation movement, and the AIDS crisis. In 1991, however, police brutality toward African Americans returned to the headlines with the videotaped beating of black motorist Rodney King by white police officers in Los Angeles. King, who was intoxicated but unarmed, led police on a high-speed chase before they managed to pull him over. After King exited his vehicle, the officers knocked him to the ground and then kicked him and clubbed him with their batons more than 50 times. A witness recorded the arrest with a camcorder and submitted the video to a local news station. It was one of the first incidents of police brutality to be captured on video, and it generated shock and outrage across the country.

Tensions had been rising in Los Angeles between the police force and residents of low-income, predominantly black neighborhoods for some time. Under Chief Daryl Gates, the Los Angeles Police Department had taken a hard-line, aggressive approach to controlling gang activity, drug trafficking, and violent crime. Some black residents resented the stepped-up enforcement, which they claimed encouraged racial profiling and police brutality. "What we had was aggressive paramilitary policing with a culture that was mean and cruel, racist, and abusive of force in communities of color, particularly poor communities of color,"[9] said civil rights lawyer Connie Rice. When the four police officers who had beaten King were acquitted despite the video evidence, the city erupted in riots that left 60 people dead and caused an estimated $1 billion in property damage. The violence caused school closures, suspension of mass transit and mail service, and cancelation of professional sports contests until the National Guard finally restored order. Similar incidents of police violence toward unarmed black men—many of them captured on video— inspired BLM protests and sparked urban riots a quarter-century later.

Hip-Hop Culture

Discontent with conditions in African American communities and demands for racial equality have long found cultural expression in music, art, literature, film, fashion, and sports. Some of the most powerful and influential representations of the problems commonly faced by urban black youth have come from hip-hop culture, and particularly rap music. "We attended horrible schools, lived in neighborhoods of squalor, but now we had a voice," wrote Taymullah Abdur-Rahman. "Hip-hop is really a lifestyle that consists of more than just music; there's graffiti, there's dancing, there's social justice, and there's personal style and agency. You don't have to be from the hood to be hip-hop but you do have to be authentic and you must have respect for the past."[10]

Historians have compared rap music to the storytelling tradition of African griots, who preserved and recounted village histories in music or prose. "Rappers are viewed as the voice of poor, urban African-American youth," Stanford University historian Becky Blanchard noted. "They are the keepers of contemporary African-American working-class history and concerns." Rap music has also been described as a means of political protest against economic inequality and racial oppression. "Rap has developed as a form of resistance to the subjugation of working-class African-Americans in urban centers," Blanchard wrote. "Though it may be seen primarily as a form of entertainment, rap has the powerful potential to address social, economic, and political issues and act as a unifying voice for its audience."[11]

Hip-hop culture influenced the BLM movement in several ways, including its commitment to voicing the concerns of black youth, its emphasis on uncompromising blackness, and its refusal to tone down its message in an effort to gain mainstream acceptance or respectability. "I think what Black Power did, and what hip-hop would pick up on later, was move away from the sort of passive sense of suffering, 'We shall overcome,'" said Todd Boyd, author of *The New H.N.I.C.: The Death of Civil Rights and the Reign of Hip Hop*. "Hip-hop is much more active, much more aggressive, much more militant." Like rap artists, BLM activists have modernized old tools for a new era and employed language—in the form of trending hashtags, slogans, memes, and reportage on social media—to raise public awareness of police violence and other issues. "Hip hop is inherently political, the language is political," Boyd stated. "It uses language as a weapon—not a weapon to violate or not a weapon to offend, but a weapon that pushes the envelope that provokes people, makes people think."[12]

The Dream of a Postracial Society

For many Americans, the 2008 election of Barack Obama as the nation's first black president seemed to signal the arrival of a promising new era in race relations. Obama's ascendance to the highest political office in the land suggested that the United States had overcome its long history of racial discrimination and finally become a place where all people, as King had famously dreamed, would "not be judged by the color of their skin, but by the content of their character."[13] After decades of struggle by generations of activists, African Americans appeared to have gained access to the full rights, protections, and benefits of citizenship.

Many black activists viewed Obama's election as the culmination of their efforts and thought their days of street protests were over. Yet hopes that the nation now offered equal rights and opportunities to all citizens were quickly dashed. "I think many people wish to believe that the civil rights movement largely accomplished its goals, and that the racial nightmare is over and the dream has been achieved," sociologist Aldon Morris said. "Yes, there has been considerable change since the heyday of the civil rights movement, but . . . to claim that we are now in a post-racial society—to claim that skin color and so forth no longer matters—is to really engage in a myth that is soothing, but at the same time, does not address reality."[14]

The fierce opposition to Obama's presidency—which was manifested in partisan rancor, political obstructionism, and vitriolic hatred—forced many African Americans to reassess what it meant for the country and for their lives. They were deeply discouraged by entrenched bigotry that had yet to be overcome. "Any façade of a post-racial reality was soon melted away amid the all-consuming eight-year flame of racial reckoning that Obama's election sparked,"[15] Wesley Lowery wrote in *"They Can't Kill Us All": Ferguson, Baltimore, and a New Era in America's Racial Justice Movement.* Some observers viewed the hostile response to the first black president as consistent with a pattern that had followed significant black gains in other eras of history. "The often-racist backlash that followed Obama's election," according to Baptiste, "initiated this new generation into a cycle that has characterized America's fraught racial history: A period of optimism born out of a spectacular political moment—the Emancipation Proclamation; Reconstruction; the civil-rights movement of the 1960s—is then followed by a period of reaction and retrenchment."[16]

Meanwhile, a series of violent encounters between white police officers and unarmed black men offered stark evidence that social justice remained an elusive goal. Muhammad described policing as "the most enduring aspect of the struggle for civil rights." Although police practices such as racial profiling, harassment, and excessive use of force were familiar experiences in black communities, the problem was largely invisible to white Americans. "White people, by and large, do not know what it is like to be occupied by a police force," Muhammad stated. "They don't understand it because it is not the type of policing they experience. Because they are treated like individuals, they believe that if 'I am not breaking the law, I will never be abused.'"[17]

Although Obama's election failed to usher in a postracial era, it did help forge a new generation of black activists who were determined to confront the barriers to equality that remained in place. BLM started with loosely organized protests against police violence in a few cities and quickly expanded into a national movement with broader goals. "Black Lives Matter is often called a 'civil rights' movement. But to think that our fight is solely about civil rights is to misunderstand the fundamental aspirations of this movement," said BLM cofounder Opal Tometi. "The current struggle is not merely for reforms of policing, any more than the Montgomery Bus Boycott was simply about a seat on the bus. It is about the full recognition of our rights as citizens; and it is a battle for full civil, social, political, legal, economic, and cultural rights."[18]

Notes

1. Nathalie Baptiste, "Origins of a Movement," *Nation*, February 9, 2017, https://www.thenation.com/article/origins-of-a-movement/.
2. Elahe Izadi, "Black Lives Matter and America's Long History of Resisting Civil Rights Protesters," *Washington Post*, April 19, 2016, https://www.washingtonpost.com/news/the-fix/wp/2016/04/19/black-lives-matters-and-americas-long-history-of-resisting-civil-rights-protesters/?utm_term=.8c27d5911739.

3. Ibid.

4. "Civil Rights Activism, from Martin Luther King to Black Lives Matter," NPR, January 18, 2016, https://www.npr.org/2016/01/18/463503838/civil-rights-activism-from-martin-luther-king-to-black-lives-matter.

5. Rebecca Onion, "Four Ways We've Distorted the History of the Civil Rights Movement," *Slate*, January 15, 2018, http://www.slate.com/blogs/the_vault/2018/01/15/forgotten_aspects_of_civil_rights_history.html?wpisrc=burger_bar.

6. Michael Martin, "Black Power! Inside the Movement," NPR, April 3, 2009, https://www.npr.org/templates/story/story.php?storyId=102691304.

7. Nikole Hannah-Jones, "Yes, Black America Fears the Police. Here's Why," ProPublica, March 4, 2015, https://www.propublica.org/article/yes-black-america-fears-the-police-heres-why.

8. *Report of the National Advisory Commission on Civil Disorders* (Washington, DC: National Criminal Justice Reference Service, 1968), 1, https://www.ncjrs.gov/pdffiles1/Digitization/8073NCJRS.pdf.

9. Karen Grigsby Bates, "When LA Erupted in Anger: A Look Back at the Rodney King Riots," NPR, April 26, 2017, https://www.npr.org/2017/04/26/524744989/when-la-erupted-in-anger-a-look-back-at-the-rodney-king-riots.

10. Taymullah Abdur-Rahman, "Hip-Hop: A Child of the Civil Rights Movement," *Huffington Post*, January 26, 2016, https://www.huffingtonpost.com/taymullah-abdurrahman/hip-hop-a-child-of-the-civil-rights-movement_b_9039664.html.

11. Becky Blanchard, "The Social Significance of Rap and Hip-Hop Culture," Ethics of Development in a Global Environment (EDGE) Seminar, Stanford University, July 26, 1999, https://web.stanford.edu/class/e297c/poverty_prejudice/mediarace/socialsignificance.htm.

12. Scott Simon, "Hip-Hop: Today's Civil Rights Movement?" *NPR*, March 1, 2003, https://www.npr.org/templates/story/story.php?storyId=1178621.

13. Martin Luther King Jr., "I Have a Dream," Address Delivered at the March on Washington for Jobs and Freedom, August 28, 1963, https://kinginstitute.stanford.edu/king-papers/documents/i-have-dream-address-delivered-march-washington-jobs-and-freedom.

14. Denise Chow, "A Dream Deferred: America's Changing View of Civil Rights," LiveScience, August 29, 2013, https://www.livescience.com/39292-america-civil-rights.html.

15. Wesley Lowery, *"They Can't Kill Us All": Ferguson, Baltimore, and a New Era in America's Racial Justice Movement* (New York: Little, Brown, 2016), 14.

16. Baptiste, "Origins of a Movement."

17. Hannah-Jones, "Yes, Black America Fears the Police. Here's Why."

18. Opal Tometi, "Black Lives Matter Is Not a Civil Rights Movement," *Time*, December 10, 2015, http://time.com/4144655/international-human-rights-day-black-lives-matter/.

| # The Origin of #BlackLivesMatter

The Black Lives Matter (BLM) movement traces its history to the 2012 shooting of a black teenager named Trayvon Martin. His death ignited a polarizing national debate about racial profiling and civil rights and spurred the creation of the hashtag #BlackLivesMatter. Martin was killed in a gated community called the Retreat at Twin Lakes in Sanford, Florida, a suburb of Orlando, where his father's fiancée lived. Although Martin lived with his mother in Miami Gardens, he often visited Sanford with his father. On the dark, rainy evening of February 26, Martin—who had turned 17 a few weeks earlier—decided to walk to a nearby convenience store to buy snacks. After purchasing an AriZona fruit drink and a bag of Skittles candy, he began walking back to the home of his father's fiancée, raising the hood of his sweatshirt against the rain as he went.

Around the same time, a local resident named George Zimmerman was driving through the neighborhood. Following a series of home burglaries in the community, the 28-year-old Zimmerman had organized a neighborhood watch group to augment law enforcement patrols. The volunteer members had received training from a Sanford police officer, who had instructed them not to carry weapons and to report any suspicious activity or potential crimes to the proper authorities, rather than confronting or trying to apprehend lawbreakers themselves. When Zimmerman spotted Martin walking down the street, he dialed 911 and told the emergency dispatcher, "Hey, we've had some break-ins in my neighborhood and there's a real suspicious guy. . . . This guy looks like he's up to no good or he's on drugs or something. It's raining, and he's just walking around looking about."[1]

Meanwhile, Martin was talking on his cell phone with Rachel Jeantel, his girlfriend from Miami Gardens. At one point, he told her that a "crazy and creepy"[2] man was watching him. Jeantel expressed concern and advised Martin to run. Still on the phone with the dispatcher, Zimmerman reported that the stranger in the hoodie was coming toward him. "He's got his hand in his waistband. And he's a black male," Zimmerman stated. "Something's wrong with him. Yup, he's coming to check me out. He's got something in his hands. I don't know what his deal is. . . . These assholes, they always get away."[3] When Martin started to run, Zimmerman got out of his vehicle and chased after him. The dispatcher warned Zimmerman not to follow the suspect, telling him "We don't need you to do that,"[4] and asked him to wait for the police to arrive.

Martin initially told his girlfriend that he had lost the man who had been following him, but then he and Zimmerman ran into each other again. Jeantel recalled hearing their encounter over the phone. "Trayvon said, 'What are you following me for?' and the man said, 'What are you doing here?' Next thing I hear is somebody pushing, and somebody pushed Trayvon because the head set just fell. I called him again and he didn't answer the phone."[5] At that point, a neighbor called 911 to report hearing a struggle and a man yelling for help behind her home. The emergency dispatcher was still taking down information when a gunshot rang out. When Sanford police arrived on the scene a few minutes later, they found Martin dead of a gunshot wound to the chest.

Zimmerman admitted that he had shot the unarmed teenager with a handgun he was licensed to carry. According to his version of events, Martin had initiated the violent altercation by punching him in the face, knocking him to the ground, jumping on top of him, and slamming his head into the pavement. He had facial injuries that he said he had obtained while struggling with Martin. Zimmerman claimed that he had feared for his life and fired his gun in self-defense.

Following their initial investigation into the matter, Sanford police accepted Zimmerman's account and decided not to arrest or file criminal charges against him.

Outrage in the Black Community

Martin's parents, Tracy Martin and Sybrina Fulton, were shocked and outraged by their son's death. Describing Trayvon as a respectful, easygoing young man with no history of violence, they disputed Zimmerman's characterization of the shooting as self-defense. They pointed out that Trayvon was merely walking along and minding his own business when Zimmerman began following him. They accused Zimmerman of forming unwarranted suspicions about Trayvon on the basis of race. Martin's parents also questioned Zimmerman's decision to carry a gun while serving as a neighborhood watch volunteer, as well as his decision to exit his vehicle and pursue Trayvon on foot—both actions that violated the guidelines set forth by law enforcement officials. They insisted that their son would still be alive if not for Zimmerman's vigilantism, and they demanded that he be held accountable for his actions. "I believe the responsibility lies on him as an adult," Sybrina Fulton stated, "because my son was not following him. He did not confront him. He did not chase him. And he did not have a weapon."[6]

To draw attention to the cause, Martin's parents created an online petition calling for Zimmerman to be arrested and put on trial for killing their son. As news of the incident spread, up to 50,000 people signed the petition per hour, and it eventually collected more than 2 million signatures. Protests demanding justice for Trayvon Martin were held in dozens of cities. In the Miami area, students at 34 schools staged walkouts in a show of solidarity with Martin's family.[7] One of the largest demonstrations, known as the Million Hoodie March, took place on March 21 in New York City. Around 1,000 people—most of them wearing hooded sweatshirts—attended a rally in Union Square. "We're not going to stop until we get justice," Tracy Martin told the crowd. "My son did not deserve to die."[8]

A number of black political leaders, writers, and celebrities also expressed their feelings about the Trayvon Martin case. Professional basketball player LeBron James posted photographs of himself and his Miami Heat teammates wearing hoodies. U.S. Representative Frederica Wilson, whose Florida congressional district included Martin's home in Miami Gardens, delivered an emotional speech before Congress about the tragic consequences of racial profiling. "I am tired of burying young black boys. I am tired of watching them suffer at the hands of those who fear them and despise them," she declared. "No more, America! No more hiding your criminal racial profiling by using self-defense to get away with murder."[9] President Barack Obama called for a full investigation of the shooting in a March 23 statement. "When I think about that boy, I think about my own kids," he said. "If I had a son, he'd look like Trayvon. I think they are right to expect that all of us as Americans are going to take this with the seriousness this deserves and get to the bottom of what happened."[10]

As more information came to light about Zimmerman's background, critics charged that his actions were driven by an obsession with crime and law enforcement. Sanford police released transcripts of 46 calls Zimmerman had made to 911 dispatchers over the previous eight years. Although some of the calls concerned mundane matters like potholes, trash collection, and excessive noise, a number of them reported the presence of black men on foot in the neighborhood. Martin's supporters argued that Zimmerman regarded all black men as potential criminals who posed a threat to his community. Robert Zimmerman, George's father, called the media characterizations "misleading" and denied that his son had targeted Martin on the basis of race. He told a newspaper that his son's ethnicity was Hispanic, and that as a minority George "would be the last to discriminate for any reason whatsoever."[11] Robert Zimmerman also criticized black leaders for overreacting to the case. "I never foresaw so much hate coming from the president, the Congressional Black Caucus, the NAACP," he stated. "Every organization imaginable is trying to get notoriety or profit from this in some way."[12]

A number of conservative media figures weighed in to defend Zimmerman. They argued that he had a legal right to carry a weapon and was justified in using it to protect himself from bodily harm. Some of Zimmerman's defenders portrayed Martin as a troublemaker who got what he deserved. When conservative news sites learned that Martin had been suspended from school for 10 days, for instance, they implied that he had been disciplined for aggressive or violent behavior.

In reality, school authorities had found a plastic baggie containing traces of marijuana in the teen's backpack during a routine check. A few conservative bloggers accompanied their posts about Trayvon Martin with photographs of an older black man in a menacing pose to bolster their claims that the teenager was a thug. Fox News commentator Geraldo Rivera ignited controversy by asserting that Martin's clothing choices contributed to his death. "His hoodie killed Trayvon Martin as surely as George Zimmerman did," he wrote. "Trayvon was unarmed save his box of Skittles. But his hoodie gave his assailant cause to think him the enemy."[13] Rivera later apologized for his comments.

Racial Profiling and Stand Your Ground Laws

The rising tide of protests garnered attention in the news media and commentary on social media. A CNN blog noted that the incident had "in many ways turned into a full-scale moment of reflection for Americans, of all races, as to whether we as a nation have moved forward in our quest for equality among races."[14] Under intense public pressure and federal scrutiny, the Sanford Police Department finally arrested Zimmerman on April 11, nearly two months after the shooting. He was charged with second-degree murder, which required prosecutors to prove that Zimmerman had acted with evil intent when he killed Martin, as well as manslaughter, a lesser charge that only required prosecutors to prove that Zimmerman had knowingly put himself in a situation that led to Martin's death.

When the case went to trial in July 2013, a great deal of debate focused on the broad protections for gun rights and self-defense provided under Florida law. The state had been one of the first in the nation to pass a "shall-issue" statute removing most of the restrictions on citizens seeking to obtain licenses to carry concealed weapons. In 2005, Florida adopted a controversial "stand-your-ground" law, allowing citizens to use deadly force in self-defense. Unlike more stringent laws in other states, the Florida law did not require citizens to attempt to avoid or retreat from a potentially dangerous situation before resorting to deadly force. Critics charged that the law made police reluctant to investigate any shooting in which the shooter claimed self-defense because it was nearly impossible to convict the person of a crime. When such cases reached trial, the defendant only had to show that a reasonable person would have felt threatened in the same situation, whereas the prosecution had to prove beyond a reasonable doubt that the shooter did not act in self-defense. However, a cosponsor of the legislation, Florida Representative Dennis Baxley, argued that the law did not apply in Zimmerman's case. "There's nothing in this statute that authorizes you to pursue and confront people, particularly if law enforcement has told you to stay put," he said. "I don't see why this statute is being challenged in this case. That is to prevent you from being attacked by other people."[15]

The Zimmerman trial lasted three weeks. After hearing all of the evidence, the jury—which was comprised of six women—received the following instructions: "If George Zimmerman was not engaged in an unlawful activity and was attacked in any place where he had a right to be, he had no duty to retreat and had the right to stand his ground and meet force with force, including deadly force if he reasonably believed that it was necessary to do so to prevent death or great bodily harm to himself or another or to prevent the commission of a forcible felony."[16] After deliberating for 16 hours over two days, the jury reached a verdict on July 13. They found Zimmerman not guilty on both charges. Later interviews revealed that the jurors felt conflicting witness statements and a lack of clear evidence had created reasonable doubt as to who had instigated the fatal altercation. Even though Zimmerman had apparently pursued Martin against police advice, the jury decided that the shooting was justified under Florida's stand-your-ground law.

Response to Zimmerman's Acquittal

Protesters outside the courthouse expressed shock and despair upon hearing that Zimmerman had been acquitted of all charges. Daryl Parks, an attorney and spokesman for Martin's parents, said the family was devastated but wanted to move forward. "There was always a possibility that this jury could do the unthinkable," he said. "Although we accept the verdict, we find it to be socially illogical and that's why so many people have outrage. No decent thinking person would ever believe that an armed person should ever be allowed to shoot an unarmed child."[17] Marches and rallies took place in Los Angeles, New York, Miami, and many other cities over the next few days. Obama and other black leaders encouraged the protesters to avoid violence, which they said could only lead to further tragedies. "I know this case has elicited strong passions. And in the wake of the verdict, I know those passions may be running even higher," the president stated. "But we are a nation of laws, and a jury has spoken. I now ask every American to respect the call for calm reflection from two parents who lost their young son."[18]

At the same time, some commentators expressed satisfaction with the verdict and asserted that justice had been served. To a large extent, the response to Zimmerman's acquittal was shaped by race. An ABC News–*Washington Post* poll found that 86 percent of African American respondents were dissatisfied with the verdict, compared to 31 percent of white respondents. "I think it's important to recognize that the African American community is looking at this issue through a set of experiences and a history that doesn't go away," Obama explained. "And that ends up having an impact in terms of how people interpret the case."[19] On social media, however, reaction to the verdict was overwhelmingly negative. A Pew Research analysis of nearly 5 million Twitter comments posted the day after Zimmerman's trial concluded found that tweets opposing his acquittal outnumbered posts supporting it by a four-to-one margin.[20]

Alicia Garza, a labor organizer in Oakland, California, learned of Zimmerman's acquittal while sitting in a crowded bar with her husband and two friends. Garza had a long-standing interest in racial justice and a younger brother the same age as Trayvon Martin, so she had followed the case closely. When the verdict was announced, Garza noticed that voices in the noisy bar suddenly fell silent, and many black patrons began walking out as if in a daze. At home, Garza struggled to process her feelings. "The one thing I remember from that evening, other than crying myself to sleep that night, was the way in which as a black person, I felt incredibly vulnerable, incredibly exposed and incredibly enraged," she recalled. "We were carrying this burden around with us every day: of racism and white supremacy. It was a verdict that said: black people are not safe in America."[21]

As Garza gauged reactions to the verdict on social media, she saw two main themes emerging in the black community. Some people said they were disgusted by Zimmerman's acquittal but not surprised. They argued that the criminal justice system had always been corrupt and biased against people of color, so there was no reason to expect a different outcome. Others said Martin's tragic death offered lessons that black people should heed in order to live safely in white society. "So, that's why we need to vote, that's why we need to pull our pants up, that's why we need to give our kids better educations, that's why our kids should not be wearing hoodies," Garza explained. "All of these things, you know, blaming black people for systems and social dynamics that we did not create."[22]

Garza rejected these notions in a passionate message that she posted on Facebook. She argued that black people should not accept blame for becoming victims of violence or adjust their appearance and behavior to appear more respectable to white people. She also criticized the expectation that Zimmerman would be acquitted. "Stop saying we are not surprised. That's a damn shame in itself," she wrote. "I continue to be surprised at how little black lives matter. And I will continue that. Stop giving up on black life." Garza concluded her post with a heartfelt expression of support for the black community: "Black people. I love you. I love us. Our lives matter."[23]

Patrisse Cullors, a fellow advocate for social justice, was moved and inspired by Garza's Facebook message. Cullors turned her friend's sentiments into a hashtag, #BlackLivesMatter, and shared the post. The two women reached out to another activist, Opal Tometi, to discuss ways of using the anger and anguish generated by the Trayvon Martin verdict to mobilize people. "The phrase 'Black Lives Matter' resonated with me on a very deep level," Tometi recalled. "It seemed simple enough, but it was also a demand and a critique of our system that was very poignant and clear. It went from looking at just the interpersonal instances of racism to the structural."[24] Tometi created a social media platform around the hashtag and encouraged people to share their views about why black lives matter. Many people adopted the slogan as a powerful expression of support and call to action for the black community. As Garza described the fledgling movement, "Black Lives Matter is an ideological and political intervention in a world where Black lives are systematically and intentionally targeted for demise. It is an affirmation of Black folks' contributions to this society, our humanity, and our resilience in the face of deadly oppression."[25]

Notes

1. "Audio: Calls from Zimmerman, Neighbor Capture Last Minutes of Martin's Life," *Washington Post*, May 20, 2012, http://www.washingtonpost.com/wp-srv/special/nation/last-minutes-trayvon-martin-911-calls/index.html.

2. Jonathan Capehart, "Trayvon Martin's Mother: 'You Can't Justify It.'" *Washington Post*, February 26, 2013, https://www.washingtonpost.com/blogs/post-partisan/wp/2013/02/25/trayvon-martins-mother-you-cant-justify-it-2/?utm_term=.2fc0870fa3f0.

3. "Audio: Calls from Zimmerman, Neighbor Capture Last Minutes of Martin's Life."

4. Ibid.

5. Matt Gutman and Seni Tienabeso, "Trayvon Martin's Last Phone Call Triggers Demand for Arrest 'Right Now,'" ABC News, March 20, 2012, http://abcnews.go.com/US/trayvon-martin-arrest-now-abc-reveals-crucial-phone/story?id=15959017.

6. Capehart, "Trayvon Martin's Mother: 'You Can't Justify It.'"

7. Sarah Gonzalez, "Students at 34 Miami Schools Walk Out of Class for Trayvon Martin," StateImpact, March 24, 2012, https://stateimpact.npr.org/florida/2012/03/24/students-at-34-miami-schools-walk-out-of-class-for-trayvon-martin/.

8. Jared T. Miller, "Million Hoodie March in New York City Rallies Support for Trayvon Martin," *Time*, March 22, 2012, http://newsfeed.time.com/2012/03/22/million-hoodie-march-in-new-york-rallies-support-for-trayvon-martin/.

9. Matt Stopera, "Florida Representative Frederica Wilson's Emotional Speech about Trayvon Martin's Shooting," BuzzFeed, March 22, 2012, https://www.buzzfeed.com/mjs538/florida-representative-frederica-wilsons-emotiona?utm_term=.xf5VGNGPR#.bd420K0k1.

10. Adam Serwer, "The Right Goes Nuts over Obama's Trayvon Comments," *Mother Jones*, March 23, 2012, http://www.motherjones.com/crime-justice/2012/03/obama-comments-trayvon-martin-case-and-right-goes-nuts/.

11. Elizabeth Flock, "Who Is George Zimmerman?" *Washington Post*, March 21, 2012, https://www.washingtonpost.com/blogs/blogpost/post/who-is-george-zimmerman-more-information-emerges-about-the-shooter-of-trayvon-martin/2012/03/21/gIQA6muiRS_blog.html?utm_term=.8a6b6aae6d70.

12. Lucy Madison, "George Zimmerman's Father: 'So Much Hate' Coming from Obama," CBS News, March 29, 2012, https://www.cbsnews.com/news/george-zimmermans-father-so-much-hate-coming-from-obama/.

13. Geraldo Rivera, "Trayvon Martin Would Be Alive but for His Hoodie," Fox News, March 23, 2012, http://www.foxnews.com/politics/2012/03/23/trayvon-martins-hoodie-and-george-zimmerman-share-blame.html.

14. "Trayvon Martin Case Sparks Dialogue on Racial Inequality, Meaning of Justice," CNN, March 22, 2012, http://news.blogs.cnn.com/2012/03/22/

trayvon-martin-case-sparks-dialogue-on-racial-inequality-meaning-of-justice/comment-page-19/?hpt=hp_c1.

15. Marc Caputo, "Stand Your Ground Fathers: Trayvon Martin's Killer Should Likely Be Arrested," *Miami Herald*, March 20, 2012, http://miamiherald.typepad.com/nakedpolitics/2012/03/stand-your-ground-fathers-trayvon-martins-shooter-should-likely-be-arrested-doesnt-deserve-immunity.html.

16. Marc Caputo, "Juror: We Talked Stand Your Ground before Not-Guilty Zimmerman Verdict," *Miami Herald*, July 16, 2013, http://www.miamiherald.com/news/state/florida/trayvon-martin/article1953286.html.

17. Richard Luscombe, "George Zimmerman Acquittal Leads to Protests across U.S. Cities," *Guardian*, July 15, 2013, https://www.theguardian.com/world/2013/jul/15/trayvon-martin-protests-streets-acquittal.

18. David Jackson, "Obama's Statement on Trayvon Martin," *USA Today*, July 15, 2013, https://www.usatoday.com/story/theoval/2013/07/15/obama-trayvon-martin-statement/2517025/.

19. Jon Cohen, "Race Shapes Zimmerman Verdict Reaction," *Washington Post*, July 22, 2013, https://www.washingtonpost.com/politics/race-shapes-zimmerman-verdict-reaction/2013/07/22/3569662c-f2fc-11e2-8505-bf6f231e77b4_story.html?utm_term=.e8c6707cd254.

20. Mark Jurkowitz and Nancy Vogt, "On Twitter: Anger Greets the Zimmerman Verdict," Pew Research Center, July 22, 2013, http://www.pewresearch.org/fact-tank/2013/07/17/on-twitter-anger-greets-the-zimmerman-verdict/.

21. Elizabeth Day, "#BlackLivesMatter: The Birth of a New Civil Rights Movement," *Guardian*, July 19, 2015, https://www.theguardian.com/world/2015/jul/19/blacklivesmatter-birth-civil-rights-movement.

22. Melissa Harris-Perry, "Why #BlackLivesMatter's Alicia Garza Won't Support Hillary Clinton," *Elle*, June 27, 2016, http://www.elle.com/culture/career-politics/news/a37416/alicia-garza-black-lives-matter-hillary-clinton/.

23. Jelani Cobb, "The Matter of Black Lives," *New Yorker*, March 14, 2016, https://www.newyorker.com/magazine/2016/03/14/where-is-black-lives-matter-headed.

24. Emily Ramshaw, "A Black Lives Matter Co-Founder on Surveillance and Social Media," *Coveteur*, February 23, 2017, http://coveteur.com/2017/02/23/opal-tometi-co-founder-black-lives-matter-social-media-power/.

25. Alicia Garza, "A Herstory of the #BlackLivesMatter Movement," *Feminist Wire*, October 7, 2014, http://thefeministwire.com/2014/10/blacklivesmatter-2/.

CHAPTER THREE

From Social
Media to the
Streets of
Ferguson

#BlackLivesMatter remained primarily a hashtag on social media for more than a year after George Zimmerman was acquitted for killing Trayvon Martin. In the summer of 2014, though, organizers took their message to the streets of Ferguson, Missouri, where a white police officer fatally shot another unarmed black teenager. The relationship between black citizens and law enforcement in the St. Louis suburb had long been characterized by tension and mistrust. Although 67 percent of Ferguson's 21,000 residents were black, 50 of the city's 53 police officers were white.[1] The situation erupted on August 9, 2014, after 18-year-old Michael Brown was shot and killed by Officer Darren Wilson.

The shooting occurred in the early afternoon on Canfield Drive, a quiet street in the Canfield Green apartment complex. Wilson was driving through the low-income, mostly black neighborhood in his patrol car responding to a report of a theft that had occurred at a nearby convenience store. He saw Brown and his friend Dorian Johnson walking down the middle of the street, noticed that they fit the description of the suspects, and stopped to question them.

Conflicting reports have created uncertainty about what happened next. Wilson claimed that Brown reached through the window of the patrol car, punched him in the face, and tried to take away his gun. Johnson claimed that Wilson grabbed his friend by the neck and pulled him through the window of the police car. Wilson fired his gun twice during the struggle, and then Brown moved away from the car and began running down the street. The officer exited the vehicle, pursued Brown a short distance on foot, and then discharged his weapon 10 more times. An autopsy showed that Brown was struck by at least six bullets, including two that hit his head.

According to Wilson, he shot Brown in self-defense when the teenager turned around to confront him and placed his hand near his waist, as if to pull out a gun. Johnson's version of events differed. He claimed that his friend had turned around to surrender to the police officer and had his hands up when he was shot. The confrontation between Wilson and Brown attracted the attention of passersby on the street and residents in nearby apartments, and their accounts of the shooting varied as well. Some witnesses said Brown was running away and had his back to Wilson when he was killed, while others said the officer had stood over the teen and shot him while he was lying on the ground.

A crowd soon gathered at the scene, and rumors spread quickly as people posted photos, videos, and anguished messages on social media. While Ferguson police investigated the shooting, Brown's body remained face down in the street in a puddle of blood for more than four hours. Some witnesses were traumatized by the gruesome sight, while others were enraged by what they viewed as disrespect for the dead boy and his family. Given the long-standing animosity between Ferguson's black community and law enforcement, some residents viewed it as a threatening gesture by the police. "For some, first in Ferguson and later around the nation, the spectacle of Brown's body cooling on the asphalt conjured images of the historic horrors of lynchings—the black body of a man robbed of his right to due process and placed on display as a warning to other black residents,"[2] journalist Wesley Lowery wrote in his book *They Can't Kill Us All*.

Police investigators eventually covered Brown with a sheet and cordoned off the block. By that time, Brown's parents and other family members had arrived, along with local reporters. After workers from the county medical examiner's office finally removed the body, the crowd followed Brown's grief-stricken mother, Lezley McFadden, down

Canfield Drive to the spot where her son had died. "They had tried to wash his blood from the street with soap and water but it was still there,"[3] recalled Johnetta "Netta" Elzie, who grew up near Canfield Green and arrived on the scene within hours of the shooting. Elzie soon emerged as one of the most prominent citizen journalists to chronicle the events happening in Ferguson in real time on Twitter. "I was doing what everyone should be doing if you say that you love where you're from and your people," she explained. "It just so happens that black people get killed by the police often here and I was tired of it."[4]

Vigils and Protests

On August 10, local church leaders organized a vigil on Canfield Drive that was attended by dozens of Brown's friends and family members. Concerned citizens also held peaceful demonstrations outside the Ferguson police headquarters. Many people expressed anger about the shooting and the handling of the investigation afterward. Protesters demanded that the police provide a full explanation of what happened and issue an official apology for leaving Brown's body in the street for so long. They also wanted the officer responsible to be identified and held accountable for his actions. Based on reports that Brown had raised his hands in surrender before he was shot, many protesters used that gesture and carried signs with the slogan "Hands Up, Don't Shoot!"

In addition to demanding justice for Brown, many black residents of Ferguson brought up wide-ranging accusations of racial profiling, harassment, and abuse they had suffered at the hands of the city's police force. "Residents described Mike Brown as a symbol of their own oppression," Lowery wrote. "Brown's death afforded an opportunity through protest for otherwise ignored voices to be heard."[5] That evening, the peaceful protests gave way to violent unrest. Vandals smashed car windows and looted stores and businesses. A gas station located a block from the site of the shooting went up in flames. Ferguson police responded in riot gear and eventually managed to disperse the crowd.

The following day, city officials asked protesters to confine their activities to daylight hours in order to reduce the risk of vandalism and violence. The demonstrations continued and remained peaceful until August 13, when a group of protesters refused to disperse at nightfall. Ferguson police responded by firing tear gas canisters into the crowd. "I just couldn't believe that the police would fire tear gas into what had been a peaceful protest," said activist DeRay Mckesson. "I was running around, face burning, and nothing I saw looked like America to me."[6] Among the people targeted by tear gas was a news crew, and their footage helped bring the standoff in Ferguson to national attention.

On August 15, Ferguson police identified Wilson as the officer involved in the shooting. At the same time, they released a surveillance video from a nearby convenience store depicting Brown's activities shortly before he was killed. The teenager appeared to pick up a box of cigars and start to walk out without paying. When the cashier tried to stop him, Brown appeared to push the man into a display case. Ferguson Police Chief Tom Jackson said the video showed that Wilson had probable cause to stop and question the teen as a suspect in the reported robbery.

Brown's family reacted angrily to the release of the video, arguing that the police were trying to justify Wilson's actions by shifting blame onto the victim. Regardless of Brown's activities earlier that day, they insisted that deadly force was unnecessary since the teenager was unarmed at the time of the shooting. They countered the portrayal of Brown as a criminal by noting that the young man had worked hard to earn his high school diploma and was planning to attend classes at a vocational school. His uncle, Bernard Ewing, asserted that Brown would never have attacked Wilson because he had warned his nephew not to confront the Ferguson police under any circumstances. "I let him know like, if the police ever get on you, I don't care what you doing, give it up," he said. "Because if you do one wrong move, they'll shoot you. They'll kill you."[7]

The controversy surrounding the release of the surveillance video spilled over into the streets of Ferguson. The demonstrations remained peaceful yet insistent during the daytime hours, but the atmosphere changed when darkness fell, with each night getting progressively more violent. Rioters threw rocks, bricks, and bottles, started fires, looted stores, and destroyed property. In response, the Ferguson police response grew increasingly militarized, confronting residents with armored trucks, assault weapons, rubber bullets, and tear gas. Countless images and videos documented the tense struggle for control of the city streets. Although Missouri Governor Jay Nixon imposed a curfew between the hours of midnight and 5:00 a.m., many people defied the order. Finally, on August 18, National Guard troops arrived to quell the unrest and restore order to Ferguson.

The Black Lives Matter Freedom Ride

The Ferguson protests received a great deal of national media coverage, which drew the attention of black activists in other cities. Alicia Garza, whose Facebook message had inspired the hashtag #BlackLivesMatter, recalled feeling sick when she saw photos of Michael Brown's dead body on television. Patrisse Cullors, who had created the hashtag, said scenes from the streets of Ferguson reminded her of iconic images from the civil rights movement of the 1960s that showed unarmed protesters being beaten by police officers wielding billy clubs or threatened by snarling police dogs. Both women longed to do something to support the protesters as well as raise awareness of the fact that the problems of racially biased policing and state-sanctioned violence toward black people were not limited to Ferguson.

The idea of organizing a Freedom Ride to bring activists from across the country to Ferguson originated with Darnell L. Moore, a black scholar and writer from New Jersey. Like Garza and Cullors, he was haunted by Brown's death and alarmed by the forceful police response to the protests. They worked together to create a plan of action under the banner of Black Lives Matter (BLM). "We used our lists of email addresses and various networks to pull people together. We reached out to our friends, really," Moore recalled. "Within a few days, we had a national team of volunteers. Patrisse mentioned that we already have this Black Lives Matter hashtag in place and that we should use it. Alicia gave us the passwords to all the social media outlets for the hashtag, and before we knew it, we had some 500 people across the country riding to Ferguson!"[8]

Participants in the BLM Freedom Ride to Ferguson came from 18 different cities and represented all walks of life, including students, journalists, doctors, lawyers, engineers, and pastors. Many sought to expand the local movement that was seeking justice for Michael Brown into a national movement seeking social justice for all black Americans. "The BLM Ride was organized in the spirit of the early 1960s interstate Freedom Rides in the racially segregated South," Cullors explained. "The ride was a call to action for black people and their allies to fight for justice—not just for Brown and his family, but for all of us."[9]

Once the Freedom Ride buses reached Ferguson in late August, BLM activists joined forces with activists from other organizations, such as Hands Up, Don't Shoot, Missourians Organizing for Reform and Empowerment, and the Organization for Black Struggle. They participated in protest marches while carrying banners with the phrase "Black Lives Matter," and they attended strategy sessions aimed at resolving problems in Ferguson as well as expanding the message nationally. The meetings resulted in a list of demands that included placing Wilson under arrest, appointing a special prosecutor to oversee the case, demilitarizing the local law enforcement response, and requiring the use of video cameras by police departments with a history of racial bias.

A Grand Jury Refuses to Indict

Meanwhile, on August 20, St. Louis County Prosecuting Attorney Robert McCulloch convened a grand jury to review evidence and decide whether Wilson should be charged with a crime in the shooting death of Brown. The panel of 12 jurors was selected randomly from citizens of the greater St. Louis area. It included six white men, three white women, one black man, and two black women. For the grand jury decision to be final, 9 of the 12 members had to reach an agreement. Over the next three months, they heard 70 hours of testimony from dozens of witnesses, examined hundreds of photographs, and evaluated information from forensic and medical experts.

Protests continued while residents of Ferguson anxiously awaited the grand jury's decision. Activists from BLM and other groups returned to the city for "Ferguson October," which was marked by a series of protest actions that included unfurling a banner at a St. Louis Symphony concert, disrupting a St. Louis Rams football game, and staging an overnight occupation of St. Louis University. A 1,000-person march to Ferguson police headquarters led by clergy from various religions resulted in the arrest of nearly 50 protesters. *New Yorker* columnist Jelani Cobb noted shifts in the tactics and focus of the protesters, writing that "an amorphous anger has evolved into a structured, organized response to an array of concerns that extend beyond the shooting itself."[10]

On November 24, McCulloch held a live news conference to announce the grand jury's findings. Concerned about the potential for a violent reaction, he first described the investigations that had been conducted by Ferguson police and the Federal Bureau of Investigation (FBI), the evidence that had been presented to the grand jury—including conflicting testimony by eyewitnesses—and the results of an autopsy, which concluded that Brown had not been shot in the back and most likely did not have his hands up. After considering all of these factors, he explained, the grand jury had not found sufficient evidence to bring charges against Wilson. Even though he was not indicted, Wilson resigned from the Ferguson police force a few days later.

Brown's family rejected the prosecutor's explanations and expressed outrage upon hearing the grand jury's verdict. Although they had previously urged protesters to avoid violence, their immediate response was to reverse that position. Brown's stepfather, Louis Head, exhorted a crowd gathered outside the police headquarters to "burn this bitch down." He later apologized, but his words generated controversy and contributed to a new eruption of unrest in Ferguson. "I think he was expressing a sentiment that a lot of folks in that crowd felt and when he said those words, the mood did change and things got a little bit out of control," said St. Louis Alderman Antonio French. "There is such anger and emotion around this case."[11] Later that night, rioters set fires that burned an entire block in Ferguson's business district.

Over the next few days, demonstrations took place in 170 cities nationwide to protest the grand jury's decision not to indict Wilson. Critics of the verdict claimed that it reflected the view of city officials and law enforcement that Brown's death was unimportant. Many protesters adopted the slogan "Black Lives Matter" to express their opposition to this view. BLM activists organized a series of die-ins, direct-action protests inspired by the sit-ins employed during the civil rights movement. On November 28, protesters disrupted busy holiday-season shopping at malls across the country by lying down on the floor as if they had been shot. Their targets included Boston, Chicago, New York, San Francisco, Washington, DC, and the Mall of America in Minneapolis. According to historian Herbert Ruffin, "These demonstrations, as with all Black Lives Matter protests, were intentionally provocative in order to draw attention to issues that were continually ignored by most non-black people."[12]

Justice Department Investigation

While the grand jury carried out its work, the U.S. Department of Justice (DOJ) launched its own investigation. In addition to determining whether Wilson had committed a crime in shooting Brown, federal investigators looked for evidence of racial bias in the operations of Ferguson's police department and municipal court system. FBI agents and civil rights attorneys spent six months in the city, conducted hundreds of interviews, reviewed thousands of documents, and observed several court sessions. U.S. Attorney General Eric Holder released a detailed report of their findings on March 4, 2015. Although federal investigators did not find grounds to charge Wilson, they identified a pattern of civil rights violations by Ferguson law enforcement and court officials toward the city's black residents.

The report found that black residents accounted for 93 percent of all arrests in Ferguson between 2012 and 2014, although they comprised only 67 percent of the city's population. Black people were far more likely than white people to be arrested for petty violations, such as walking in the road (95 percent of those charged were black), failure to comply with a police order (94 percent), and disturbing the peace (92 percent). Black drivers also accounted for 86 percent of all motorists stopped by the Ferguson police, and they were twice as likely as white drivers to be subjected to searches during traffic stops. Many of the stops and searches were conducted without probable cause or reasonable suspicion. In addition, 90 percent of documented uses of force by Ferguson police officers targeted African Americans.[13]

The DOJ report also noted that the municipal courts in Ferguson routinely imposed fines and fees on black residents for minor offenses, such as rolling through a stop sign. If a resident was unable to pay, the court would issue a warrant for their arrest. The Ferguson court system issued nearly 33,000 arrest warrants in 2013, or 1.5 for each of the city's 21,000 residents. The investigation revealed that 96 percent of the people arrested on municipal warrants were black, and black defendants were 68 percent less likely than white defendants to have their cases dismissed by a judge.[14] This situation led to a disproportionate number of black residents being held in jail. Spending time in jail often created financial hardships for residents in the form of missed wages, lost jobs, unpaid bills, and foreclosed homes.

DOJ investigators attributed the disparate treatment of black and white residents to racial bias in Ferguson's criminal justice system. They uncovered examples of openly racist e-mails and other communications among municipal employees. They noted that many of the city's policies and practices were not aimed at protecting citizens and promoting public safety, but at generating revenue at the expense of black residents by trapping them into paying fines and fees. The report concluded that Ferguson engaged in systematic racial discrimination in violation of the Fourteenth Amendment to the U.S. Constitution, which guarantees all citizens equal protection under the law. The DOJ noted that racial bias, stereotyping, harassment, and excessive force by Ferguson police contributed to an atmosphere of suspicion and distrust toward law enforcement within the city's black community.

In announcing the DOJ findings, Holder said he understood why protesters had treated Brown's death as the last straw. "Amid a highly toxic environment, defined by mistrust and resentment, stoked by years of bad feelings, and spurred by illegal and misguided practices, it is not difficult to imagine how a single tragic incident set off the city of Ferguson like a powder keg,"[15] he noted. The DOJ report led to Jackson's resignation as Ferguson Police Chief. The city eventually entered into a consent agreement that required it to make significant changes to eliminate racial bias from the operations of the police department and court system. Brown's family cited the DOJ findings in a civil wrongful death lawsuit against the city of Ferguson, former Police Chief Jackson, and Officer Wilson. They claimed that the police department's culture of hostility toward black residents had contributed to Wilson's use of excessive force. A judge agreed and awarded the family a $1.5 million settlement.

Emergence of National Movement

The events in Ferguson drew attention to wider problems of racially biased policing in the United States. Brown's father, Michael Brown Sr., expressed hope that his son's death had inspired black activism for social justice nationwide. "Mike opened the doors for those other people, if not him, to get some type of justice," he stated. "There ain't no sitting down no more or sweeping us under the carpet. We standing on top of the carpet now and letting you know that we're not taking it no more."[16]

President Barack Obama responded to the events in Ferguson by convening the Task Force on Twenty-First Century Policing in December 2014. Among the members of this group were academic experts, law enforcement officers, and civil rights activists, including Ferguson protester Brittany Packnett. Its goal was to find ways to improve the relationship between municipal police departments and the local communities they serve. In a report issued in May 2015, the task force recommended providing sensitivity training for law enforcement, conducting public reviews of police procedures and conduct, and collecting more data on police shootings and use of force.

Within a year of Brown's death, the Associated Press reported that 40 new laws had been passed in 24 states to address the treatment of citizens by law enforcement.[17] Some of the measures required police officers to wear body cameras to record their interactions with the public and limited the use of surplus military equipment by police departments. "You really haven't seen anything as impactful as we are seeing ... right now," noted policy analyst Samuel Sinyangwe, "in terms of seeing immediate legislation being proposed and passed and signed at all levels of government."[18] Change occurred more slowly in Missouri, where legislators passed only one bill—placing limits on the fines charged for traffic tickets and other municipal violations—out of 65 that were proposed in the wake of Ferguson.

Not all of the changes garnered the support of police unions and other groups representing the interests of law enforcement. Critics expressed frustration with the rush to pass legislation aimed at placating BLM protesters. "While we're trying to save lives, politicians are trying to save their jobs,"[19] said Jim Pasco, executive director of the Fraternal Order of Police. They argued that most police officers were dedicated public servants who risked their lives to protect people from harm. They charged that protesters focused only on the small number of tragic mistakes by law enforcement rather than the large number of positive actions. That also asserted that the media and black activists were wrong to assume that all policing problems had a racial component.

In addition to igniting a national debate about policing, the Ferguson protests launched BLM to prominence as one of the most visible and organized of the new generation of civil rights groups. The hashtag was used on Twitter more than 2 million times during those chaotic weeks. "Ferguson would birth a movement and set the nation on a course for a still-ongoing public hearing on race," Lowery wrote. "The social justice movement spawned from Mike Brown's blood would force city after city to grapple with its own fraught histories of race and policing. As protests propelled by tweets and hashtags spread under the banner of Black Lives Matter and with cell phone and body camera video shining new light on the way police interact with minority communities, America was forced to consider that not everyone marching in the streets could be wrong."[20]

Notes

1. Denver Nicks, "How Ferguson Went from Middle Class to Poor in a Generation," *Time*, August 18, 2014, http://time.com/3138176/ferguson-demographic -change/.
2. Wesley Lowery, *"They Can't Kill Us All": Ferguson, Baltimore, and a New Era in America's Racial Justice Movement* (New York: Little, Brown, 2016), 25.
3. Aaron Randle, "Now You See Me: A Look at the World of Activist Johnetta Elzie," *Complex*, March 8, 2016, http://www.complex.com/life/2016/03/ johnetta-elzie-profile.
4. Hillary Crosley Coker, "Activist Johnetta Elzie Talks Ferguson and Black Lives Matter," *Jezebel*, July 17, 2015, https://jezebel.com/activist-johnetta -elzie-talks-ferguson-black-lives-ma-1718374170.
5. Lowery, *"They Can't Kill Us All": Ferguson, Baltimore, and a New Era in America's Racial Justice Movement*, 16.
6. Jay Caspian Kang, "Our Demand Is Simple: Stop Killing Us," *New York Times*, May 4, 2015, https://www.nytimes.com/2015/05/10/magazine/our-demand -is-simple-stop-killing-us.html.
7. John Eligon, "Michael Brown Spent Last Weeks Grappling with Problems and Promise," *New York Times*, August 24, 2014, https://www.nytimes.com/2014/

08/25/us/michael-brown-spent-last-weeks-grappling-with-lifes-mysteries
.html.

8. Monica J. Casper, "Black Lives Matter: A Conversation with Patrisse Cullors and Darnell L. Moore," *Feminist Wire*, December 1, 2014, http://thefeministwire.com/2014/12/black-lives-matter-black-life-matters-conversation-patrisse-cullors-darnell-l-moore/.

9. Patrisse Cullors, "Five Ways to Never Forget Ferguson—And Deliver Real Justice for Michael Brown" (blog), November 29, 2015, http://patrissecullors.com/2015/11/29/5-ways-to-never-forget-ferguson-and-deliver-real-justice-for-michael-brown/.

10. Jelani Cobb, "Ferguson October: A Movement Goes on Offense," *New Yorker*, October 15, 2014, https://www.newyorker.com/news/news-desk/ferguson-october.

11. Ray Sanchez, "Michael Brown's Stepfather at Rally: 'Burn This Bitch Down,'" CNN, December 8, 2014, http://www.cnn.com/2014/11/25/us/michael-brown-stepfather-video/index.html.

12. Herbert Ruffin, "Black Lives Matter: The Growth of a New Social Justice Movement," Black Past, 2017, http://www.blackpast.org/perspectives/black-lives-matter-growth-new-social-justice-movement.

13. Jon Swaine, "Ferguson Mired in Sweeping Racial Discrimination, Federal Report Finds," *Guardian*, March 3, 2015, https://www.theguardian.com/us-news/2015/mar/03/justice-department-racial-discrimination-ferguson-police.

14. Ibid.

15. "Ferguson Unrest: From Shooting to Nationwide Protests," BBC News, August 10, 2015, http://www.bbc.com/news/world-us-canada-30193354.

16. Mukul Devichand, "Will Black Lives Matter Change America in an Election Year?" BBC News, January 30, 2016, http://www.bbc.com/news/blogs-trending-35444899.

17. David A. Lieb, "Ferguson Spurs Forty New State Measures; Activists Want More," Associated Press, August 3, 2015, https://apnews.com/2cd834a26ad146ceb04ba6f265566ec5/ferguson-spurs-40-new-state-measures-activists-want-more.

18. "Michael Brown's Family Receives $1.5 Million Settlement in Wrongful Death Lawsuit," CBS News, June 23, 2017, https://www.cbsnews.com/news/michael-brown-ferguson-missouri-settlement-wrongful-death-lawsuit/.

19. Lieb, "Ferguson Spurs Forty New State Measures; Activists Want More."

20. Lowery, *"They Can't Kill Us All": Ferguson, Baltimore, and a New Era in America's Racial Justice Movement*, 13.

CHAPTER FOUR

The Movement Gains Force

After the Ferguson protests took Black Lives Matter (BLM) from social media to the streets, the next challenge for activists was to use the momentum they had generated to forge an organization and expand the fight for social justice and civil rights nationwide. Some BLM leaders described their task as turning a moment into a movement. The three women who had popularized the hashtag worked with other activists to build BLM into a decentralized, member-led network that comprised dozens of local chapters. They rejected the top-down, hierarchical structure employed by the civil rights organizations of earlier eras in favor of a collective leadership model. "We've always made it clear that we are one of many," said Ferguson activist Johnetta Elzie. "There's not one person who can be a leader of the movement. We're all leaders."[1]

Some critics questioned the decentralized approach, arguing that the lack of a visible, charismatic spokesperson in the tradition of Martin Luther King Jr. would deprive the BLM movement of meaning and focus. But the organizers worried that relying on a strong central leader would cause BLM to fall apart if the individual viewed as the face of the movement were discredited or assassinated. They also felt that establishing a hierarchical structure would mean disempowering ordinary people, especially marginalized populations such as low-income people, LGBTQ people, and people with disabilities. Maintaining decentralized, collective leadership, on the other hand, had the potential to produce creative, cutting-edge campaigns to address specific local problems. "Our goal," the organizers explained on the BLM website, "is to support the development of new black leaders, as well as create a network where black people feel empowered to determine our destinies in our communities."[2]

As a member-led, grassroots movement, BLM sometimes struggled to convey its identity and message. Each chapter developed its own goals, organized its own demonstrations, and coordinated with activists in the larger BLM network through social media. This approach held appeal for many young people, who tended to "march to the beat of different civic drum than earlier generations," according to the 2016 study *Beyond the Hashtags*, "preferring individually-motivated, digitally-enabled, cause-based activism to the more top-down, institution-centered, adult-directed civic styles of yesteryear."[3] In the absence of a single, focused media presence, however, some observers questioned what the group was trying to accomplish. "Most of the folks in the movement are young and we're black so they assume we're uneducated and uninformed and we're just angry and in the streets,"[4] Elzie acknowledged. When peaceful protests veered out of control and resulted in rioting and vandalism, some critics blamed BLM's lack of organizational guidance and clear rules of engagement. Even though BLM did not sanction violence, such incidents reflected on the group and affected the way it was viewed by white society. "When something tragic happens, we're all blamed because there's no central leadership," Elzie said. "We all take a hit."[5]

Many observers noted contrasts between the BLM protests and civil rights actions of the 1960s. Whereas antisegregation marches and sit-ins were typically led by well-dressed, educated, respectable ministers who advocated nonviolent resistance, the front lines in Ferguson and later BLM actions often featured black women, poor and working-class youth, and LGBTQ individuals. The anger, fearlessness, and radicalism of their protests dramatically altered the image of black activism from earlier eras. "They keep wanting to put us in the civil rights movement box," Elzie stated. "And we're not in that box. We're not respectable enough to be that. People didn't change who they were when they came outside. No church told us to go. No organization told us to go. There was no start button. People saw what happened to Mike Brown and . . . we just went."[6]

From the beginning, BLM modeled and advocated inclusion. The organization's guiding principles, published on its website, emphasize respecting and celebrating differences in sexual orientation, gender identity, economic status, immigration status, ability or disability, age, and religion. The BLM movement was founded by three black women, two of whom (Alicia Garza and Patrisse Cullors) identify as queer. Unlike the civil rights movement, which largely relegated women to the background, BLM expressly affirms black women, embraces female leadership, and seeks to dismantle patriarchal attitudes and institutions. "It has historically been the case that racial justice has been only thought to be the work of black men," said Ferguson Freedom Ride organizer and LGBTQ rights activist Darnell L. Moore. "Our history has conveniently invisibilized black women and queer and trans people. . . . But if the mantra of this [group] is 'black life matters,' it's important to us to emphasize that *all* black lives matter. This is an opportunity to expand a racial justice framework in an equitable way that includes all of us."[7]

On its website, BLM defines its mission as providing "an ideological and political intervention in a world where black lives are systematically and intentionally targeted for demise," as well as "an affirmation of black folks' contributions to this society, our humanity, and our resilience in the face of deadly oppression." Its guiding principles include commitments to securing freedom and justice for black people, creating a world without racism, and ensuring that black people have social, economic, and political power. In addition, the organization encourages members to build a supportive and nurturing black community and to view themselves as part of a global black family. Finally, activists in the BLM movement "are unapologetically black in our positioning. In affirming that Black Lives Matter, we need not qualify our position. To love and desire freedom and justice for ourselves is a prerequisite for wanting the same for others."[8]

More Police-Involved Deaths, More Protests

As the mission and principles of the BLM network coalesced, local groups continued calling for justice in cases where black men and boys were killed by police officers. One of the most high-profile incidents occurred in Staten Island, New York, on July 17, 2014—a few weeks before Michael Brown was shot in Ferguson. Several New York Police Department (NYPD) officers confronted Eric Garner, a 43-year-old father of six children, on a busy sidewalk and accused him of selling loose cigarettes illegally. Garner argued with the officers and demanded that they leave him alone. Instead, they decided to place him under arrest. Officer Daniel Pantaleo grabbed Garner by the neck and wrestled the 350-pound man to the ground. Pantaleo straddled Garner and maintained a chokehold restraint, in violation of NYPD policy, while other officers held him down and applied handcuffs. Garner, who had asthma, said "I can't breathe" 11 times before he lost consciousness. A bystander with a cell phone captured the incident on video.

Garner's death came to national attention in early December, when a Staten Island grand jury decided not to indict Pantaleo. The verdict was announced a little over a week after the Ferguson verdict, which fueled a growing sense of outrage over what appeared to be a pattern of white police officers using deadly force against unarmed black men and not being held accountable for their actions. Tens of thousands of pro-testers marched through New York City, many of them chanting "I Can't Breathe," and demonstrations of solidarity took place in cities across the country. In a speech, New York City Mayor Bill de Blasio expressed sympathy for Garner's family and support for the BLM move-ment, admitting that he worried about the safety of his biracial son in encounters with law enforcement. "This is now a national moment of grief, a national moment of pain," he stated. "You've heard in so many places, people of all backgrounds, utter the same basic phrase. They've said 'Black Lives Matter.' And they said it because it had to be said. It's a phrase that should never have to be said—it should be self-evident. But our history, sadly, requires us to say that Black Lives Matter."[9]

Meanwhile, another controversial police shooting occurred in Cleveland, Ohio, on November 22, 2014. Tamir Rice, a 12-year-old black boy, was playing with a pellet gun in a park near his home, which prompted another park visitor to call 911. Although the caller noted that the person in question appeared to be a juvenile and that the gun was "probably fake," the dispatcher did not relay this information to the responding officers. A surveillance video showed a patrol car arrive on the scene and Officer Timothy Loehmann leap out of the vehicle, draw his weapon, and shoot Rice twice in the abdomen from a distance of less than 10 feet. Although Loehmann fired within two seconds of his arrival, he claimed that the boy had ignored a warning to show his hands and had instead lifted his shirt as if to pull out a gun from his waistband. Loehmann and his partner failed to provide medical attention to Rice as he lay bleeding on the ground for four minutes before an ambulance arrived, and the boy died in a hospital the next day.

The Rice case turned out to be another in which a grand jury declined to bring criminal charges against a police officer responsible for the death of a black youth. The prosecutor who presented the case to the grand jury argued that the shooting was a reasonable response to the circumstances and that civilians should not question the split-second, life-or-death decisions police officers were forced to make. Civil rights activists rejected his reasoning. "This case is one of the most egregious examples of how the criminal justice system routinely fails in ensuring accountability for the needless killing of unarmed civilians at the hands of police," declared Janai Nelson of the National Association for the Advancement of Colored People (NAACP) Legal Defense Fund. "Rather than 'a perfect storm of human error' as Cuyahoga County Prosecutor Timothy McGinty described this tragedy, Rice's death and the lack of accountability for it are a result of racial profiling, incompetent 911 services, over-zealous and reckless policing practices, and a systemic bias in favor of police."[10] Loehmann was eventually fired from the police force for lying on his job application, and Rice's family received a $6 million wrongful death settlement from the city.

Another shooting occurred on April 4, 2015, in North Charleston, South Carolina. Walter Scott, a 50-year-old black man, was pulled over by white police officer Michael Slager because his car had a broken taillight. After stopping on the side of the road, Scott got out of the vehicle and ran, possibly because he was afraid of being arrested for unpaid child support. Slager drew his weapon and shot the unarmed man several times in the back as he was running away, and a witness recorded the incident on video. In this case, however, the officer was fired from the police force and indicted on both state and federal murder charges. In addition, the incident prompted the South Carolina legislature to pass a law requiring police officers to wear body cameras to record their interactions with the public.

A week later, on April 12, 25-year-old Freddie Gray fled from Baltimore police. After catching him, several officers restrained Gray on the ground by kneeling on his back and neck. They arrested him on a weapons charge for carrying a knife, shackled his hands and feet, and threw him head first into the metal-lined rear compartment of a police van. The van made several stops before reaching the police station, during which witnesses claimed that Gray was screaming or moaning in pain. Gray lapsed into a coma and was taken to a hospital, where he died a week later of severe spinal injuries that he had sustained while in police custody. BLM activists blamed police brutality for Gray's death. Over the next few weeks, Baltimore was rocked by a series of protests that often erupted into riots. Hundreds of businesses were looted or damaged, 250 people were arrested, and more than 20 police officers were injured before National Guard troops were called in to quell the unrest. Although six police officers were eventually charged with crimes or misconduct, three were acquitted and all charges were dropped against the others.

Responding to these and other instances of police violence, BLM chapters organized more than 950 demonstrations between August 2014 and August 2015.[11] Each new protest attracted media coverage, increased public awareness, and spurred more people to take action, thus fueling the growth of the movement. By drawing attention to the sheer number of police-involved deaths of unarmed black men, however, the BLM protests also contributed to feelings of fear and helplessness among some African Americans. "The outrages in this bloody vein of twisted American culture, becoming more prevalently understood with each videotaped incident of police and their brutal over-responses to black citizens, continue to stoke unshirted fear and anger," wrote black columnist Stephen Henderson. "For many people like me, the trend is no longer inspiring a 'when will this stop' response, but an eerie and unsettling resignation to 'when will this happen to someone I know?'"[12]

Sandra Bland and #SayHerName

As the BLM movement grew, it also expanded its focus to include resisting police brutality aimed at black women. Although incidents involving unarmed black men received most of the media attention in the early years of the movement, BLM activists identified 70 cases in which black women and girls were killed by police officers between 2012 and 2014. "We know the story of marginalized people, of repressed people in America, is often one of erasure," said activist Brittany Packnett. "And when you talk about not only being a person of color but a woman on top of that, you can feel that erasure doubly."[13]

Many of the women were killed around the same time, and sometimes in the same cities, as police-involved deaths of black males that generated massive protests. Twenty-two-year-old Rekia Boyd was shot and killed by an off-duty Chicago police officer on March 22, 2012—less than a month after Trayvon Martin—after he confronted her group of friends in a park. Forty-seven-year-old Yvette Smith was shot and killed by a Texas deputy on February 16, 2014—six months before Michael Brown—as she opened the front door of a friend's house after calling 911 to report a domestic disturbance. Tanisha Anderson, a 37-year-old mother with bipolar disorder, died on November 13, 2014—nine days before Tamir Rice—when police responding to her family's request for help dealing with a manic episode forcibly restrained her in the street outside her Cleveland home. These stories did not become national news, however, and few people other than dedicated local activists were aware of them. "I think the problem is male domination of police departments, of the media, of government," said David Malik, an attorney representing Anderson's family. "The combination of being a woman, being an African American, sometimes being poor, or sometimes having a police record means such individuals never even make it on the radar screen."[14]

This situation began to change in 2015, when the African American Policy Forum (AAPF) launched the #SayHerName campaign to document, publicize, and seek justice in cases of police violence against black women. "Although black women are routinely killed, raped, and beaten by the police, their experiences are rarely foregrounded in popular understandings of police brutality," explained AAPF executive director Kimberlé Crenshaw. "Yet, inclusion of black women's experiences in social movements, media narratives, and policy demands around policing and police brutality is critical to effectively combating racialized state violence for black communities and other communities of color."[15] The AAPF sponsored a vigil in New York City on May 20, 2015, in memory of all the black women and girls who had been killed by police. They used the hashtag #SayHerName to remember the victims, tell their stories, and expand the discourse of the BLM movement to include women.

The issue came to the forefront of the BLM movement two months later, when a black female social justice advocate named Sandra Bland died in a jail cell in Waller County, Texas. Bland was pulled over by Texas State Trooper Brian Encinia on July 10 for failing to signal a lane change. She argued with the officer and refused to extinguish her cigarette and step out of her vehicle. Encinia then violated procedure by threatening her with his Taser, forcing her out of the car, pinning her to the ground, and slamming her head into the pavement. The arrest was captured on the patrol car's dashcam video as well as a cell-phone video filmed by a bystander. Bland later told a friend on the phone that she had been "roughed up" and planned to press charges against the officer. Three days after she was arrested, Bland was found dead in her cell. The police claimed that she had committed suicide by hanging herself with a plastic garbage bag, but her family and friends disputed that claim. They said there was no indication that she was suicidal, and they questioned inconsistencies in reports, statements, and videos from her time in police custody.

BLM and other groups organized protests and demanded an independent investigation into Bland's death. Many activists viewed the circumstances as suspicious and believed that Bland may have been killed by the police. They questioned why Bland had been arrested and held in jail over a minor traffic violation, and they criticized both Encinia and jail personnel for violating police procedures. Encinia was eventually fired from the state police force for lying to investigators, but a grand jury declined to indict him. Bland became a key figure in the emerging #SayHerName campaign, as protesters put her name and photo on signs and websites as a symbol of police violence against black women. The case aroused controversy, however, as critics dismissed Bland's death as a suicide and accused protesters of promoting conspiracy theories. "Some in the Black Lives Matter movement have become so attached to the narrative of rampant police brutality against black Americans that they cannot accept a tragic death that does not have a uniformed villain," wrote conservative columnist Ian Tuttle. "They need Sandra Bland to have been strangled by police; it's the only thing that supports their worldview."[16]

The Mapping Police Violence Project

With the growth of the BLM movement, activists increasingly encountered critics who claimed that they exaggerated the prevalence of police violence against black people. Even though the U.S. Department of Justice (DOJ) had uncovered evidence of rampant racial discrimination in the Ferguson Police Department, some people contended that the shooting of Michael Brown was an isolated incident rather than part of a nationwide pattern. BLM organizers found it difficult to refute such claims without hard evidence, yet few official sources collected information specifically about police violence.

Data analyst Samuel Sinyangwe set out to address this problem by creating a map of all the police-involved deaths occurred in cities across the United States. "In the aftermath of Ferguson, there was this big question, 'Is this a pattern, is this an isolated incident?'" he related. "There are statistics on all kinds of violent crimes. And yet, when it comes to people being killed by police officers, there's no data on that. So a light bulb went off in my head."[17] Sinyangwe and a team of social justice activists combed through police reports, newspaper stories, crowd-sourcing databases, and other resources. They compiled the information to create an interactive website called Mapping Police Violence.

The data revealed that black people were three times more likely to be killed by police than white people in the United States. In addition, 69 percent of the black people killed by police in 2014 were unarmed and not suspected of committing a violent crime.[18] "Ferguson is everywhere," Sinyangwe stated. "All over the country you're seeing black people being killed by police."[19] Yet in 99 percent of the police-related deaths that occurred in 2015, no officers involved were convicted of a crime. In response to BLM protests over the lack of police accountability, the DOJ investigated police misconduct in a number of large cities, including Baltimore, Cincinnati, Cleveland, New Orleans, Portland, New York, Seattle, and St. Louis.

Data collected by Sinyangwe and his associates disproved critics' assertion that higher crime rates in black communities explained why police violence disproportionately affected black people. The Mapping Police Violence project compared the cities of Buffalo, New York, and Orlando, Florida, which had similar characteristics in terms of overall population, racial composition, and violent crime rates. Zero civilians were killed by Buffalo police between 2013 and 2016, however, while 15 civilians were killed by Orlando police.[20] BLM activists attributed the difference to improvements in police training, priorities, and cultures.

Information from the Mapping Police Violence project supports the idea that certain reform measures can reduce the use of excessive or deadly force. Sinyangwe joined forces with activists DeRay Mckesson and Brittany Packnett to launch Campaign Zero, which offers a slate of proposed policy actions for state and local governments to take toward eliminating police violence. Solutions that have proven effective in various cities include encouraging officers to employ all other possible means before shooting, providing training in de-escalation tactics, banning choke holds, requiring officers to issue warnings prior to shooting, and requiring officers to intervene to prevent the use of excessive force. Some communities have also shifted their approach away from "for-profit policing" (issuing tickets and making arrests) and toward protecting and serving the public. In Camden, New Jersey, for instance, officers are encouraged to patrol neighborhoods on foot and build relationships with people in the community. This approach, along with community oversight and representation, has been shown to help eliminate racial bias and promote fair and impartial law enforcement.

Increasing Recognition and Influence

By early 2016, the hashtag #BlackLivesMatter had been used on Twitter nearly 12 million times, making it one of the most popular social issues ever discussed on the platform. It outlasted a number of other hashtags that referred to individual incidents—such as #HandsUpDontShoot for Michael Brown and #ICantBreathe for Eric Garner—and emerged as "a means of unifying seemingly isolated incidents into a single, affirmative demand: that black life be treated as inherently valuable,"[21] Julia Carrie Wong wrote in *San Francisco Weekly*. The phrase also extended beyond social media and protest banners to infiltrate popular culture. In addition to appearing on bumper stickers, t-shirts, and coffee mugs, it was featured in episodes of popular television series like *Law and Order* and *Empire*. The American Dialect Society even designated the slogan as its "word of the year." "What began as an outraged and grief-stricken response to one particular tragedy ultimately became how the country talked to itself about race and police brutality," Wong noted.

As BLM moved to the forefront of the modern civil rights movement, it also expanded its focus beyond police violence to encompass broader forms of discrimination affecting black communities in the United States. "Everybody is now aware of Black Lives Matter, for the most part . . . but it doesn't mean systemic racism has been eradicated," said movement cofounder Alicia Garza. "We have said from the very beginning that our movement is about . . . the fact that there isn't much quality of life for black people in this country. . . . We know that it's not isolated—that it's intentional and that it's systematic."[22] Many BLM activists launched new organizations focusing on specific issues of interest, such as poverty, unsafe housing, failing schools, or the mass incarceration of black men. Many of the smaller groups operated under the umbrella of the BLM movement and coordinated their activities with BLM chapters through social media.

On July 24, 2015, more than 2,000 activists from across the country gathered at Cleveland State University with the goal of forging a united front and articulating a common vision for the disparate groups involved in the BLM movement. They formed a coalition called the Movement for Black Lives that included the BLM network and 50 smaller groups. In 2016, the Movement for Black Lives released a political platform aimed at achieving the liberation of black communities in the United States. Its list of demands went beyond ending police violence to include securing reparations for slavery and other harms inflicted on black people, promoting investment to improve education and health in black communities, and providing black citizens with the tools and resources they needed to obtain economic justice, political power, and community control. With the release of its platform, BLM completed its transition from a social media hashtag to an influential organization and movement. As the Movement for Black Lives website explained, "Our history has taught us that we must create our own agenda, we must implement it, and we must hold elected leaders accountable to following through."[23]

Notes

1. John Blake, "Is Black Lives Matter Blowing It?" CNN, August 2, 2016, http://www.cnn.com/2016/07/29/us/black-lives-matter-blowing-it/index.html.
2. "Herstory," Black Lives Matter, n.d., https://blacklivesmatter.com/about/herstory/.
3. Deen Freelon, Charlton D. McIlwain, and Meredith D. Clark, "Beyond the Hashtags: #Ferguson, #BlackLivesMatter, and the Online Struggle for Offline Justice," Center for Media and Social Impact, February 2016, http://cmsimpact.org/wp-content/uploads/2016/03/beyond_the_hashtags_2016.pdf.
4. Blake, "Is Black Lives Matter Blowing It?"
5. Ibid.
6. Aaron Randle, "Now You See Me: A Look at the World of Activist Johnetta Elzie," *Complex*, March 8, 2016, http://www.complex.com/life/2016/03/johnetta-elzie-profile.
7. Akiba Solomon, "Get on the Bus: Inside the Black Lives Matter 'Freedom Ride' to Ferguson," *Colorlines*, September 5, 2014, https://www.colorlines.com/articles/get-bus-inside-black-life-matters-freedom-ride-ferguson.
8. "What We Believe," Black Lives Matter, n.d., https://blacklivesmatter.com/about/what-we-believe/.
9. Bill de Blasio, "Transcript: Mayor de Blasio Holds Media Availability at Mount Sinai United Christian Church on Staten Island," NYC.gov, December 3, 2014, http://www1.nyc.gov/office-of-the-mayor/news/542-14/transcript-mayor-de-blasio-holds-media-availability-mt-sinai-united-christian-church-staten.
10. Perry Bacon Jr., "Tamir Rice Decision Illustrates Power and Limits of Black Lives Movement," NBC News, December 29, 2015, https://www.nbcnews.com/meet-the-press/tamir-rice-decision-illustrates-power-limits-black-lives-movement-n487106.
11. Herbert Ruffin, "Black Lives Matter: The Growth of a New Social Justice Movement," Black Past, 2017, http://www.blackpast.org/perspectives/black-lives-matter-growth-new-social-justice-movement.
12. Stephen Henderson, "Black Lives, Tamir Rice, and America's Uncivil History," *Detroit Free Press*, December 28, 2015, https://www.freep.com/story/opinion/columnists/stephen-henderson/2015/12/28/black-lives-tamir-rice-and-americas-uncivil-history/77998986/.
13. Michelle Dean, "Black Women Unnamed," *Guardian*, June 5, 2015, https://www.theguardian.com/us-news/2015/jun/05/black-women-police-killing-tanisha-anderson.
14. Ibid.
15. Kimberlé Crenshaw, "#SayHerName Initiative," AAPF, n.d., http://www.aapf.org/sayhername/.
16. Ian Tuttle, "Evidence Doesn't Seem to Matter to #BlackLivesMatter Conspiracy Theorists," *National Review*, July 27, 2015, http://www.nationalreview.com/

article/421668/evidence-doesnt-seem-matter-blacklivesmatter-conspiracy -theorists-ian-tuttle.

17. "Why Do U.S. Police Keep Killing Unarmed Black Men?" BBC News, May 26, 2016, http://www.bbc.com/news/world-us-canada-32740523.

18. Mapping Police Violence, 2017, https://mappingpoliceviolence.org/.

19. "Why Do U.S. Police Keep Killing Unarmed Black Men?"

20. Mapping Police Violence.

21. Julia Carrie Wong, "The Bay Area Roots of Black Lives Matter," *San Francisco Weekly*, November 11, 2015, http://www.sfweekly.com/news/the-bay-area -roots-of-black-lives-matter/.

22. Elle Hunt, "Alicia Garza on the Beauty and Burden of Black Lives Matter," *Guardian*, September 2, 2016, https://www.theguardian.com/us-news/2016/ sep/02/alicia-garza-on-the-beauty-and-the-burden-of-black-lives-matter.

23. Movement for Black Lives, "About Us," n.d., https://policy.m4bl.org/about/.

CHAPTER FIVE

The Role of Social Media

A major factor in the emergence of the Black Lives Matter (BLM) movement was activists' use of Internet technology, especially social media platforms such as Twitter, Instagram, and Facebook. Social media played a vital role in BLM's growth and helped thrust the issue of racially biased policing into the national spotlight. "It's social media as much as any individual person that's responsible for transforming police brutality from a gripe in the civil rights community to a persistent, urgent topic of national dialogue,"[1] Jenée Desmond-Harris wrote in *Vox*. BLM activists used social media to share videos, images, and text narratives documenting police violence against black people. In many cases, their raw footage and commentary directly contradicted the accounts of events offered by law enforcement officials or mainstream news media. BLM organizers also used social media to build a community of like-minded activists, disseminate messages, organize protests, and coordinate actions in real time.

Leaders of the civil rights movement of the 1960s used the media to influence public opinion about segregation, voting rights, and other issues. Powerful photographs and news footage of police in riot gear confronting peaceful, unarmed protesters generated support for the passage of landmark civil rights legislation. Yet they lacked the sophisticated tools that twenty-first-century activists have at their disposal. "The thing about [Martin Luther] King or Ella Baker is that they could not just wake up and sit at the breakfast table and talk to a million people," said activist DeRay Mckesson, who has that many followers on Twitter. "The tools that we have to organize and to resist are fundamentally different than anything that's existed before in black struggle."[2]

"Black Twitter"

Using social media to spread the message of BLM was an obvious choice for the movement's founders—Alicia Garza, Patrisse Cullors, and Opal Tometi—because it offered them access to a large audience of young black users. Among African American Internet users between the ages of 18 and 29, according to a 2014 survey by the Pew Research Center, 96 percent reported using social networking sites—compared to 90 percent of white people in the same age group. Twitter was a particularly popular platform among young black people, attracting 40 percent of users, compared to only 28 percent among young white people.[3] Since young blacks make up a disproportionately large share of Twitter users, they wield a great deal of influence over the trending topics of discussion on the platform. Social scientists coined the term "Black Twitter" to describe this cultural phenomenon.

Black Twitter refers to a large, decentralized, loosely coordinated network of Twitter users whose online interactions are characterized by shared language and cultural references that are not always familiar to outside observers. Hashtags that appear on Black Twitter often accumulate into trending topics due to the size and interconnectedness of the network. Although the conversations often revolve around style, entertainment, or inside jokes, Black Twitter has also been used to raise public awareness of racism, police brutality, and other issues of importance to the black community. "Black Twitter is part cultural force, cudgel, entertainment, and refuge. It is its own society within Twitter," Soraya Nadia McDonald wrote in the *Washington Post*. "Perhaps the most significant contribution of Black Twitter is that it increases visibility of black people online, and in doing so, dismantles the idea that white is standard and everything else is 'other.' It's a radical demand for acceptance by simply existing—or sometimes dominating—in a space and being yourself, without apology or explanation."[4]

Even before the emergence of BLM, Black Twitter proved to be an influential force for social change. In 2013, for instance, activists tweeting critical remarks under trending hashtags succeeded in pressuring feminist singer Ani DiFranco to cancel a retreat that was scheduled to be held at a former slave plantation, convincing an Internet service provider to fire an executive who tweeted a racist comment, and forcing a publisher to terminate a book deal with a member of the jury in the Trayvon Martin murder trial. These high-profile cases demonstrated the power of Black Twitter to draw national attention to racial issues and generate momentum for change.

During the 2014 protests in Ferguson, Missouri, BLM activists harnessed the power of Twitter to report details about the fatal shooting of Michael Brown, organize demonstrations in the streets, record confrontations between protesters and law enforcement, and comment on events as they happened. At first, the conversations were organized under a number of different hashtags, including #Ferguson, #HandsUpDontShoot (because some witnesses claimed Brown raised his hands before he was shot), #NoJusticeNoPeace, and #BlackLivesMatter. Taken together, they made Ferguson the most-discussed topic of the year on Twitter. Supporters of the movement fired off 3.4 million tweets on November 24 alone—the day when the St. Louis County prosecutor announced that a grand jury had declined to indict Ferguson Police Officer Darren Wilson.[5]

Over time, #BlackLivesMatter outlasted other, situation-specific hashtags to become the predominant one used by social justice activists demanding attention to police violence. It expressed a compelling idea in a concise manner and provided a durable, all-purpose means of organizing conversations. "It's a very simple principle and it's not tied to any specific action. While it's focused on police shooting, it doesn't only incorporate that," said Charlton McIlwain, author of an academic study on social media usage in the BLM movement. "Something about it has broad resonance."[6] Usage of the #BlackLivesMatter hashtag increased from an average of 725 tweets per day during the second half of 2014 to more than 10,000 tweets per day in first half of 2015.[7] It eventually spread beyond activist circles to become a global phenomenon. By March 2016, it had appeared in 11.8 million tweets since Cullors used it for the first time in 2013.[8]

Controlling the Narrative

For many BLM activists, one of the primary advantages of social media was that it gave them an opportunity to circulate their own narrative of events. When an incident of police violence occurred, they did not have to wait for law enforcement officials or mainstream news outlets to provide information. Instead, they exchanged eyewitness accounts on social media. Mckesson, who joined the BLM movement during the Ferguson protests, credited social media for giving the black community a voice in stories that affected them. "As marginalized people, we have always faced erasure: either our story is never told, or it is told by everyone but us. If not for Twitter and Instagram, Missouri officials would have convinced you . . . that we simply did not exist. Or that we were the aggressors, rather than the victims. That we, and not they, were the violent ones," he wrote. "But social media was our weapon against erasure. It is how many of us first became aware of the protests and how we learned where to go, or what to do when teargassed, or who to trust. We were able to both counter the narrative being spun by officials while connecting with each other in unprecedented ways. . . . Social media allowed us to become our own storytellers. With it, we seized the power of our truth."[9]

In many cases, the accounts from protesters challenged or contradicted the version of events provided by the media. While television networks covering the Ferguson protests aired footage of rioters looting stores, for instance, real-time tweets by people on the scene described police in riot gear firing tear gas and rubber bullets into groups of peaceful protesters. A similar situation occurred in Baltimore in April 2015, during protests over the death of Freddie Gray from spinal injuries he sustained while in police custody. Local resident Kwame Rose was upset by what he viewed as inaccurate and inflammatory media reports, which largely ignored the issues raised by peaceful protesters. "When the media started saying 'tensions were high,' they were lying,"[10] Rose told the *Guardian*. The reports contradicted his experience on the streets, where he had witnessed protesters and police officers joining hands in prayer.

Rose expressed his concerns about media bias to conservative talk show host Geraldo Rivera, who was in Baltimore to cover the protests for Fox News. "You're not here reporting about the boarded-up homes and the homeless people," he declared. "You're not reporting about the poverty levels up and down North Avenue.... You're here for the 'black riots.' You're not here for the death of Freddie Gray."[11] Dramatic video of Rose's confrontation of Rivera went viral on social media, which raised awareness of BLM activists' perspective and created pressure for more balanced coverage.

Providing Visual Evidence

Social media also served as an avenue for the dissemination of compelling visual images that bolstered the BLM message about racial injustice. An eyewitness photograph of Officer Darren Wilson standing over Michael Brown's dead body—which Ferguson officials claimed had never happened—was retweeted 41,600 times on Twitter. Shocking images of confrontations between Ferguson protesters and law enforcement also grabbed public attention when they appeared on social media. A pair of images that presented peaceful civil rights protesters of the 1960s alongside Ferguson protesters, showing black activists from both eras facing militarized police, received 46,500 retweets.[12]

After Ferguson launched the BLM movement, the incidents of police violence against black citizens that received the most attention were those that were captured in photographs or videos. The death of Eric Garner, who said "I can't breathe" numerous times as he was restrained in a choke hold by New York City police, was recorded on video by a bystander with a cell phone. The video itself was retweeted 27,650 times, while a photograph of Garner with his family received 29,750 retweets.[13] These powerful images generated outrage over his death and increased the energy of BLM protests when the officers responsible were not indicted.

A study conducted by the Center for Media and Social Impact noted that the issue of police brutality "is extremely well-suited to Internet-based activism. Unlike wealth or income inequality, police brutality is concrete, discrete in its manifestations, and above all, visual. Hashtagged names and other digital memorials remind the public of the irreplaceable losses felt by the victims' families. The frighteningly common occurrence of these killings means that activists and journalists have no shortage of occasions to discuss the issue. And the video and photographic evidence that is often available provokes public outrage and disgust, at times leads to solidarity. This in turn increases the number of sympathetic ears that policy proposals intended to end police brutality ultimately reach."[14]

One prominent Twitter campaign focused on how the media portrayed black victims of police violence. Following the death of Trayvon Martin, for instance, some commentators claimed that his hoodie made him appear suspicious and menacing. A photograph of Michael Brown that appeared on many conservative news sites was taken from below, which drew attention to his intimidating size, and showed him glowering at the camera and making a gesture that some people interpreted as gang-related. Critics pointed out that other photographs of Brown were available, including one that showed him as a baby-faced teenager wearing headphones and a high school varsity jacket. Such discrepancies formed the basis of a Twitter campaign with the hashtag #IfTheyGunnedMeDown. Thousands of black users posted contrasting images of themselves side by side and asked which photo would more likely be chosen to accompany the news story if they were killed by police. "This was a way of saying 'Hey, mainstream media, you're doing something really bad! Here's this pattern, what are you going to do about it?'" explained media expert Ethan Zuckerman. "Social media is a place where people feel they can move the wheel, and they're right—they can change the representation of a gun victim in mainstream media."[15]

Raising Awareness and Organizing Resistance

Social media also enabled BLM activists to inform and educate casual observers about the issue of police violence toward African Americans. Chris Hayes, a white journalist who hosts a news program on MSNBC, relied on Twitter to enhance his understanding of the fatal shooting of Michael Brown and the Ferguson protests. He followed a number of prominent black activists and citizen journalists in order to gain insights for his viewers. "If you didn't have Black Twitter blowing up the story on social media, I don't know if it ever would have gotten this kind of momentum," he acknowledged. "That's definitely the first place I saw it. I think that's how it grabbed the attention of national media."[16] In a few cases, photos and videos on social media depicting police violence prompted conservative critics of BLM to reevaluate their unconditional support for law enforcement and call for the incidents to be investigated.

Social media also provided a forum for BLM activists to connect the dots between incidents of police violence that occurred in various cities. "Social media has been critical in the knitting together of a national narrative of police violence and abuse," said Keeanga-Yamahtta Taylor, a professor of African American studies. "Before, these incidents were depicted as isolated and individual. Social media platforms have shown how they are part of a generalized and pervasive pattern of police abuse."[17] By creating a coherent story out of separate events, the BLM movement forced the larger society to recognize the structural issues underlying racial bias in policing. "We have been holding a mirror up to the nation. And we've shown what has been going on for a very long time: that we are being brutalized," noted BLM activist Samuel Sinyangwe. "The nation is now aware of the problem. Whether we can agree on a solution or not is another question, but at least they acknowledge something is going on and that's a great first step."[18]

Finally, the BLM movement has relied on social media to build a community of committed activists and coordinate their responses to incidents of police violence. The movement can remain decentralized because activists have the ability to organize protests online, which eliminates the need for high-profile spokespeople, press conferences, and media coverage. Grassroots organizers can mobilize thousands of people quickly to exert pressure on government, law enforcement, corporations, and other institutions, hold officials accountable for their actions, and help bring about policy changes. Social media thus serves to amplify marginalized voices that might not otherwise be heard. "I can say, 'The police are literally killing us' and I've never worried whether MSNBC is watching," Mckesson said. "Because America's watching, and that's more important to me."[19]

Experiencing the Downsides

While Internet technology and social media platforms like Twitter have been powerful tools for BLM activists, they have also been employed by opponents of the movement. Critics have used social media to spread negative stories and images about victims of police violence in an effort to vilify and reduce public sympathy for them. In the case of Michael Brown, for instance, detractors publicized rap lyrics he had composed that featured violent or vulgar content, and they shared copies of a security video that appeared to show him shoving a convenience-store clerk shortly before he died.

Opponents of BLM also used social media to criticize protesters or characterize them as lawless rioters who incited violence. During a July 2016 BLM protest in Dallas, Texas, a sniper killed five white police officers and wounded seven others. Although the gunman was black and said he was seeking revenge for officer-involved killings of black citizens, he was not formally associated with BLM or any other organization. Nevertheless, detractors attacked BLM on social media, describing it as a hate group and claiming that it was responsible for the shootings because it had generated antipolice sentiment. Whereas mentions of BLM on Twitter were 87 percent positive and 11 percent negative prior to the Dallas shootings, the tenor of the discussion shifted to 28 percent positive and 39 percent negative in the 10 days afterward.[20]

Opponents also used the Internet and social media to insult, harass, and threaten BLM activists. They mined activists' social media profiles for personal information, such as cell phone numbers, home addresses, or family members' names, in order to intimidate them or disrupt protests. They also trolled activists' Twitter feeds and posted antagonistic or offensive comments. In 2015, when Mckesson attended a memorial service for nine black church leaders who were killed by a white supremacist gunman in Charleston, South Carolina, he became the focus of an angry Twitter campaign with the hashtag #GoHomeDeRay. Mckesson later estimated that he had blocked at least 15,000 people from interacting with him on Twitter.[21]

Many BLM activists expressed concern about becoming vulnerable to electronic surveillance because of their reliance on Internet and cell phone technology. "I think we are going to have to be mindful on how we are surveilled, whether it be by the FBI or local law enforcement," said BLM cofounder Opal Tometi. "We have to think about how we use technology. We can't take it for granted that everything can be done online."[22] A 2017 investigation by the *Guardian* newspaper found that undercover officers with the New York City Police Department had attended BLM protests following the death of Eric Garner, infiltrated local groups, monitored the whereabouts of leaders, and gained access to private e-mail and text messages. Individual activists also became targets of surveillance. Ferguson protest organizer Johnetta Elzie found herself being met at airports and followed around cities by local police after she was labeled a high-risk "threat actor" by a national cyber and social media security firm in 2015.

Despite the potential downsides, the Internet and social media have played a key role in projecting the messages of the BLM movement. Although there is no way to measure the impact of technology or determine whether the movement could have achieved its goals without it, there is no doubt that activists maximized the utility of the resources at their disposal. According to *Wired* writer Bijan Stephan, the BLM movement "has mounted some of the most potent civil rights activism since the '60s," and "a huge reason for all this success is that, perhaps more than any other modern American protest movement, they've figured out how to marshal today's tools."[23]

Notes

1. Jenée Desmond-Harris, "Twitter Forced the World to Pay Attention to Ferguson. It Won't Last," *Vox*, January 14, 2015, https://www.vox.com/2015/1/14/7539649/ferguson-protests-twitter.
2. Bijan Stephan, "Get Up, Stand Up: Social Media Helps Black Lives Matter Fight the Power," *Wired*, October 2015, https://www.wired.com/2015/10/how-black-lives-matter-uses-social-media-to-fight-the-power/.
3. Aaron Smith, "African Americans and Technology Use," Pew Research Center, January 6, 2014, http://www.pewinternet.org/2014/01/06/african-americans-and-technology-use/.
4. Soraya Nadia McDonald, "Black Twitter: A Virtual Community Ready to Hashtag Out a Response to Cultural Issues," *Washington Post*, January 20, 2014, https://www.washingtonpost.com/lifestyle/style/black-twitter-a-virtual-community-ready-to-hashtag-out-a-response-to-cultural-issues/2014/01/20/41ddacf6-7ec5-11e3-9556-4a4bf7bcbd84_story.html?utm_term=.e2bd42fa2977.

5. Deen Freelon, Charlton D. McIlwain, and Meredith D. Clark, "Beyond the Hashtags: #Ferguson, #BlackLivesMatter, and the Online Struggle for Offline Justice," Center for Media and Social Impact, February 2016, http://cmsimpact.org/wp-content/uploads/2016/03/beyond_the_hashtags_2016.pdf.
6. Michael McLaughlin, "The Dynamic History of #BlackLivesMatter Explained," *Huffington Post*, December 26, 2016, https://www.huffingtonpost.com/entry/history-black-lives-matter_us_56d0a3b0e4b0871f60eb4af5.
7. Freelon, McIlwain, and Clark, "Beyond the Hashtags: #Ferguson, #Black-LivesMatter, and the Online Struggle for Offline Justice."
8. Emily Parker, "#BlackLivesMatter and the Power and Limits of Social Media," *Medium*, December 2, 2016, https://medium.com/@emilydparker/how-blacklivesmatter-resembles-activism-in-the-authoritarian-world-24d1200864f6.
9. DeRay Mckesson, "Ferguson and Beyond: How a New Civil Rights Movement Began—And Won't End," *Guardian*, August 9, 2015, https://www.theguardian.com/commentisfree/2015/aug/09/ferguson-civil-rights-movement-deray-mckesson-protest.
10. Elizabeth Day, "#BlackLivesMatter: The Birth of a New Civil Rights Movement," *Guardian*, July 19, 2015, https://www.theguardian.com/world/2015/jul/19/blacklivesmatter-birth-civil-rights-movement.
11. Ibid.
12. Freelon, McIlwain, and Clark, "Beyond the Hashtags: #Ferguson, #Black-LivesMatter, and the Online Struggle for Offline Justice."
13. Ibid.
14. Ibid.
15. Day, "#BlackLivesMatter: The Birth of a New Civil Rights Movement."
16. Desmond-Harris, "Twitter Forced the World to Pay Attention to Ferguson. It Won't Last."
17. Anealla Safdar, "Black Lives Matter: The Social Media behind the Movement," *Al Jazeera*, August 3, 2016, http://www.aljazeera.com/news/2016/08/black-lives-matter-social-media-movement-160803042719539.html.
18. Day, "#BlackLivesMatter: The Birth of a New Civil Rights Movement."
19. Desmond-Harris, "Twitter Forced the World to Pay Attention to Ferguson. It Won't Last."
20. Niraj Chokshi, "How #BlackLivesMatter Came to Define a Movement," *New York Times*, August 22, 2016, https://www.nytimes.com/2016/08/23/us/how-blacklivesmatter-came-to-define-a-movement.html.
21. Stephan, "Get Up, Stand Up: Social Media Helps Black Lives Matter Fight the Power."
22. Emily Ramshaw, "A Black Lives Matter Co-Founder on Surveillance and Social Media," *Coveteur*, February 23, 2017, http://coveteur.com/2017/02/23/opal-tometi-co-founder-black-lives-matter-social-media-power/.
23. Stephan, "Get Up, Stand Up: Social Media Helps Black Lives Matter Fight the Power."

CHAPTER SIX | Criticism and Backlash

As the Black Lives Matter (BLM) movement grew and gained national visibility, it also aroused more controversy. Opponents of the movement leveled a variety of charges at BLM activists. They claimed that BLM protesters were disrespectful and disruptive, that they incited violence, that they promulgated antiwhite and antipolice messages, that they failed to articulate clear policy goals, and that they reflexively blamed racism for all the problems facing black communities. Some opponents offered thoughtful criticism of BLM's strategy and tactics, some rejected the movement's premise that racial disparities posed a serious problem in American society, and some responded to its message and methods with intense vitriol and hatred. BLM sometimes struggled to maintain its focus, articulate its vision, and sustain its momentum in the face of the backlash.

Polls suggested that Americans' views on racial issues in general, and the BLM movement in particular, were deeply polarized on the basis of race and political affiliation. A 2016 survey by the Pew Research Center found that 70 percent of blacks, but only 36 percent of whites, felt that racial discrimination posed a significant barrier to success for African Americans. Likewise, 80 percent of black respondents felt that police treated African Americans unfairly, while only

33 percent of whites agreed. On the question of how far the country had come toward racial equality, 54 percent of Republicans said enough changes had already been made, while 78 percent of Democrats said more changes were needed. With regard to the BLM movement, 64 percent of white Democrats said they supported it, while 52 percent of white Republicans opposed it.[1]

Some observers argued that the election of Barack Obama as the nation's first black president in 2008, and his reelection in 2012, showed that the United States had made significant progress toward overcoming racial discrimination. Some even claimed that the country had entered a postracial era, when the color of a person's skin was no longer an important factor in determining the trajectory of his or her life. Yet BLM forcefully challenged this idea and pushed continuing problems of systemic bias and institutional racism to the forefront. BLM supporters anticipated that their efforts would provoke a backlash among people who felt comfortable with the status quo or benefited from a social order that favored whites. "While black freedom movements, including Black Lives Matter, are clearly working for what is just, the disruption that they pose to current systems is often cast by that system as problematic, even violent," wrote Melina Abdullah in the *Conversation*. "Because systems are designed to protect themselves, they utilize their vast powers to contort the messages of those who seek to challenge them. They use the laws that they created, the media that they control, and the social structures that they erected to present those who challenge them as essentially 'enemy combatants.' "[2]

Disputes over Whose Lives Matter

Some of the strongest criticism and resistance to the BLM movement has centered around its name. Opponents charge that its emphasis on black lives implies that other lives do not matter. Some critics have suggested that saying "Black Lives Matter" is inherently racist because it devalues white lives. The movement's founders insist that this perspective misrepresents the fundamental idea behind BLM. "I absolutely believe that all lives matter," declared BLM cofounder Patrisse Cullors. "But all lives is actually the aspiration. What we're seeing right now is that all lives actually don't matter, and black lives in particular. For me to say 'black lives matter' does not mean that I'm saying any other life is less valuable, or less worthy. What I'm saying is black lives also deserve justice, they deserve protection, they deserve to be loved, to be embraced, and they deserve to quite literally live."[3]

In response to the proliferation of Black Lives Matter, opponents of the movement adopted "All Lives Matter" as an alternative hashtag and slogan. Although proponents of All Lives Matter claimed that society should be colorblind and value all people equally without regard to race, the phrase was usually used to oppose BLM and diminish its explicit affirmation of black lives. David Smith wrote in the *Conversation* that All Lives Matter "erases a long past and present of systemic inequality in the U.S. It represents a refusal to acknowledge that the state does not value all lives in the same way. It reduces the problem of racism to individual prejudice and casts African-Americans as aggressors against a colorblind post-civil rights order in which white people no longer 'see race'.... Under the white understanding, talking about systemic racism is itself racist, because it conjures into existence 'racial divides' that are invisible to whites who believe themselves to be free of prejudice."[4]

Black activists argued that All Lives Matter was a diversionary tactic aimed at shifting the focus away from systemic racism that continued to impact the lives of African Americans. "The basis of 'All Lives Matter,' specifically when deployed in response to the assertion that black lives matter, is deeply flawed," said BLM cofounder Alicia Garza. "Of course, theoretically all lives should matter. But that's not the context we live in.... Black families are seven times more likely to be homeless than white families. The majority of people in prisons and jails in this country are black. One in thirteen black people are barred from voting and influencing the decisions that impact their lives. When we address the disparities facing black people, we get a lot closer to a true democracy where all lives matter."[5]

Opponents of BLM also claimed that the organization spread antipolice messages and created a hostile environment that encouraged acts of violence against law enforcement. They argued that the movement led to a "war on cops" that took the lives of dozens of police officers. One episode often mentioned by these critics occurred in New York City in December 2014. After a Staten Island grand jury declined to indict an officer who was involved in the death of Eric

Garner, a man shot and killed two New York Police Department (NYPD) officers as they sat in a patrol car, and his social media posts indicated that he viewed his actions as retribution for Garner. Although the shooter had a long criminal record and a history of mental illness, many city officials attributed the officers' deaths to the massive BLM protests that had been taking place. Patrick Lynch, president of the New York City Patrolman's Benevolent Association (PBA), declared, "There's blood on many hands tonight—those that incited violence on the street under the guise of protests, that tried to tear down what New York City police officers did every day."[6]

A number of commentators on conservative news outlets used the phrase "Blue Lives Matter" to express their concern that police were being endangered by BLM protests and to demand greater respect for law enforcement. They pointed to statistics showing that the number of police officers gunned down nationwide increased from 41 in 2015 to 64 in 2016, including 21 who were killed in ambush-style attacks. BLM supporters countered that the 2016 figure was well within the average range of annual police deaths over the previous 10 years and also represented a steep drop from the levels seen in past decades. They denied that the movement was antipolice or condoned violence. However, they also noted that members of law enforcement had killed at least 1,058 people nationwide in 2016,[7] a disproportionate number of whom were African Americans, and they vowed to continue pushing for police reform. "There will be no end to the cry of 'Black Lives Matter,' and this movement will not take on the responsibility for crimes it did not commit. Period," Jamilah Lemieux wrote in *Ebony*. "We don't have to say that 'Blue Lives Matter,' because neither society nor 'the system' has ever suggested otherwise—quite the opposite, in fact."[8]

Following several highly publicized shootings of police officers, a total of 48 "Blue Lives Matter" bills were introduced in state legislatures in 2016 and 2017.[9] Most of these bills were intended to increase penalties for crimes committed against law enforcement officers, whether by designating them as hate crimes or by automatically making perpetrators eligible for the death penalty. Critics argued that the proposed laws were redundant because all 50 states already imposed stiffer penalties for crimes committed against police officers. They also claimed that the bills would intimidate victims of police violence and make it harder to hold officers accountable for using excessive force.

Garza denounced such laws, saying that they gave police "carte blanche authority to terrorize our communities."[10] Although few states ended up passing Blue Lives Matter bills, the drive to bolster protection for law enforcement continued at the federal level under President Donald Trump, who signed an executive order in August 2017 allowing local police departments to purchase surplus military equipment, such as armored vehicles and grenade launchers. The order reversed a ban that had been issued by the Obama administration in the wake of the Ferguson protests.

Disagreements with the Old Guard of Civil Rights Activism

Some criticism of the BLM movement has come from prominent figures within the black community, including leaders of the civil rights movement of the 1960s. A number of African American leaders have expressed concern about its decentralized structure, which they claimed created confusion about the movement's message and goals. Media giant Oprah Winfrey, for instance, argued that BLM activists should propose a slate of policy changes instead of continually organizing protests in various cities. "It's wonderful to march and to protest," she said. "What I'm looking for is some kind of leadership to come out of this to say: 'This is what we want. This is what has to change, and these are the steps that we need to take to make these changes.'"[11]

In response, BLM activists noted that various chapters had released lists of demands, including prompt investigation of police-involved deaths, detailed tracking of such deaths at the federal level, demilitarization of local police departments, and creation of citizen oversight committees to ensure accountability in law enforcement. The Campaign Zero project collected the best ideas and published them online. Radley Balko, a respected journalist who covers law enforcement policy for the *Washington Post*, praised the BLM policy proposals as "practical, well-thought out, and in most cases, achievable," adding that they "will almost certainly have an impact, even if only some of them are implemented. The ideas here are well-researched, supported with real-world evidence and ought to be seriously considered by policymakers."[12]

Other influential black leaders complained that BLM lacked a charismatic spokesperson to serve as the "face" and "voice" of the organization. They argued that clear leadership was needed, particularly in times of crisis, to express the movement's point of view to the public. They also noted the absence of memorable or eloquent speeches, along the lines of Martin Luther King Jr.'s "I Have a Dream" speech at the 1963 March on Washington, to emerge from the youthful, social media–driven BLM network. "You must have leaders. A movement without accountability or responsibility is not a sustainable model," said civil rights icon and former presidential candidate Jesse Jackson. "Who is accountable, who is to rouse the troops? It can't just be social media. Leaders matter."[13] BLM activists responded that they had intentionally created a decentralized, leaderful organization that was bigger than any one person in order to empower local chapters and encourage participation by women, LGBTQ people, immigrants, and other groups whose perspectives had been marginalized in other movements.

The BLM movement also defied convention by not aligning itself with black churches, which traditionally have played a central role in community organization efforts, such as civil rights marches and voter registration drives. Although individual black churches and pastors were involved in many BLM actions, including the Ferguson protests, the movement did not seek the official support of the church. "Protesters patently reject any conservative theology about keeping the peace, praying copiously, or turning the other cheek," Brittney Cooper wrote in *Cosmopolitan*. "Such calls are viewed as a return to passive respectability politics."[14]

Some people who participated in the civil rights movement of the 1960s disagreed with certain strategies and tactics employed by the BLM movement. They viewed BLM protests as disruptive and undisciplined, in direct contrast to the dignity and decorum that characterized protests during the earlier era. "The baby boomers who drove the success of the civil rights movement want to get behind Black Lives Matter, but the group's confrontational and divisive tactics make it difficult," civil rights activist Barbara Reynolds wrote in the *Washington Post*. "At protests today, it is difficult to distinguish legitimate activists from the mob actors who burn and loot. The demonstrations are peppered with hate speech, profanity, and guys with sagging pants that show their underwear. Even if the BLM activists aren't the ones participating in the boorish language and dress, neither are they condemning it."[15]

Younger activists in the BLM movement rejected the idea that black people could protect themselves from systemic racism by adopting certain manners of speech, dress, or behavior. They argued that the problems in society were too entrenched for the old tactics to make an impact and that assertive action was necessary to bring about meaningful change. Ferguson protester Johnetta Elzie noticed the philosophical divide between generations of activists when talking with her grandparents, who were involved in the civil rights movement. "It can be frustrating to talk to someone of that age group and say, 'This is what the victim did but they didn't deserve to die,'" she noted. "There's something in respectability politics that will make those people say, 'Well, they shouldn't have done this or that,' but it's like, 'No, you know for a fact, and have lived through it, that you don't have to do anything for a police officer or a white vigilante to kill you and get away with it. You know it doesn't have to be anything other than the color of your skin.' It is unlearning that internal oppression."[16]

In some cases, discord between different generations of activists surfaced at protests or other public events. In August 2014, for instance, group of Ferguson protesters confronted Jackson in a McDonald's parking lot and angrily accused him of coming to town for publicity rather than to support the protesters. In December 2014, Elzie and other BLM activists disrupted a march in Washington, DC, organized by the Reverend Al Sharpton's National Action Network by rushing the stage, grabbing the microphone, and asserting that Sharpton did not speak for the BLM movement. In the end, though, activists from both generations agreed that they shared the same goal: making racial equality a reality in the United States. "You can see yourselves in the Black Lives Matter students; you can understand their impatience with police violence," said Charles Cobb, who served as an organizer for the Student Nonviolent Coordinating Committee (SNCC) in the 1960s. "Our issue was segregation first, then we engaged in the fight for voter registration. But what we share with the Black Lives Matter people is their impatience .... It's their future, it's their lives—just the way it was our future and our lives back in the day."[17]

Controversy Surrounding Political Tactics

Building on chapters' success in mobilizing against local politicians who did not support their goals, the BLM movement expanded into national politics during the 2016 presidential election campaign. BLM protesters disrupted campaign events and debates, demanding attention from both Democratic and Republican candidates. Their aggressive tactics divided public opinion and generated criticism from commentators across the political spectrum. Movement organizers made a conscious decision to express their point of view in a forceful manner rather than moderating their message to appeal to a wider audience. "Black people for too long have been forced to refine our message according to what is comfortable for the mainstream," activist Brittany Packnett explained. "We have made a distinctive choice not to do it."[18] Although some critics argued that this approach would make it difficult to engage people beyond their core supporters, BLM leaders were determined to conduct their fight for racial justice in an authentic manner. "I don't think it's possible to get free while you're worrying about how some white person is experiencing your fight for your freedom," Johnetta Elzie declared. "Too often people go into the spaces of oppressed people and tell them how to be free. Your job is to listen and to be engaged."[19]

The rationale for this approach grew out of the frustration many BLM activists felt toward President Obama, who often expressed sympathy and support for their cause but also urged them to avoid violence and work to change the system from within. Many BLM supporters argued that Obama should have done more to dismantle institutional racism during his two terms in office, and they resented his efforts to tone down their message and tactics. "I find it really unfortunate that the first black president that this country has ever had spends so much time chastising black people who have done more in three years to place structural racism front and center than he himself has done in eight years of being president," Garza stated. "It's fascinating to watch President Obama be subjected to blistering prejudice and racism from members of Congress and their supporters, and yet to then watch him chastise black activists and organizers for not wanting to play their version of politics."[20]

Although black voters had largely supported the Democratic Party since the civil rights movement—and polls showed that 87 percent of black registered voters identified or leaned toward the Democrats in 2012—the BLM movement did not offer unconditional support to Democratic candidates in 2016. Instead, BLM leaders repeatedly and publicly challenged them to outline specific policies to address the root causes of problems affecting African Americans, such as racial bias in policing, mass incarceration, poverty, and homelessness. "We want to ensure that these candidates will actually deal with the issues that black people face," said BLM cofounder Patrisse Cullors. "Until we hear from candidates, beyond just saying, 'Black Lives Matter'—until we hear them really address how we are continuously cut out of the American democracy, we're going to continue to shut debates down. We're going to continue to call elected officials out."[21]

Some progressives objected to the BLM strategy, claiming that it undermined Democratic candidates who were far more sympathetic to their cause than Republicans were likely to be. In response, BLM leaders argued that the Democratic Party had grown complacent about receiving black votes. They contended that too many Democratic candidates espoused the rhetoric of systemic change but then failed to follow through and confront racial inequality in a meaningful way once they were elected to office. BLM activists said that by posing uncomfortable questions in public forums, they convinced both Democratic presidential candidates, Hillary Clinton and Bernie Sanders, to add racial justice planks to their campaign platforms. "From Ferguson to Staten Island to Baltimore, the patterns have become unmistakable and undeniable," Clinton acknowledged in a campaign speech. She went on to call for "real reforms that can be felt on our streets, in our courthouses and our jails and prisons, and in communities too long neglected."[22]

BLM protesters also challenged Republican presidential candidates and disrupted campaign rallies and debates. Instead of changing their platforms to reflect the movement's concerns, however, most Republican candidates ignored, countered, or denied the BLM arguments. Several candidates—including Chris Christie, Ted Cruz, and Donald Trump—defended police officers and claimed that BLM protests inflamed racial tensions and caused disunity that weakened America. In response to debate questions about whether they agreed that Black Lives Matter, most Republican candidates instead insisted that All Lives Matter. "A lot of people feel that [Black Lives Matter] is inherently racist," Trump stated. "It's a very divisive term, because all lives matter. It's a very, very divisive term."[23] Many GOP candidates also denounced the tactics employed by BLM protesters, which ranged from quietly wearing apparel or holding signs expressing support for the movement to loudly chanting in an effort to drown out speakers with whom they disagreed. "Commandeering the microphone, and bullying people, and pushing people out of the way, I think really isn't a way to get their message across," said Republican candidate Rand Paul. "They need to go somewhere else, and they need to rent their own microphone."[24]

Some of the most violent confrontations occurred at Trump rallies, where the candidate tacitly encouraged hostility and even physical attacks in response to disruptions by protesters. At a February 2016 rally in Las Vegas, for instance, Trump responded to an interruption by telling his supporters, "You know what they used to do to guys like that when they were in a place like this? They'd be carried out in a stretcher, folks," and adding, "I'd like to punch him in the face, I tell ya."[25] The following month, Trump offered to defend supporters in court if they happened to injure a protester who was being escorted out of a rally in Warren, Michigan. "I'm not going to say Donald Trump is responsible for this. But the undertone of his campaign is very racist," said Isaiah Griffin, a protester who was physically assaulted at a Trump rally in Fayetteville, North Carolina. "He's bringing out a lot of the things that America tries to sweep under the rug that we know are still here. It's racism."[26]

Some prominent Republicans, such as former New York City Mayor Rudy Giuliani, argued that African Americans should take greater responsibility for the problems plaguing black communities instead of blaming them on racism. He said that the BLM movement ignored black-on-black crime, for instance, which claimed far more black lives than police violence. BLM activists viewed the Republican emphasis on black-on-black crime as a diversionary tactic, arguing that most violent crimes involve a perpetrator and victim of the same race because most crime victims know their assailants personally. Although Federal Bureau of Investigation (FBI) statistics showed that 90 percent of black victims of homicide were killed by other black people in 2016, the same source showed that 83.5 percent of white murder victims were killed by other white people. In addition, the statistics showed that rates of violent victimization were twice as high among people with incomes below the federal poverty level—whether black or white—than among people with higher incomes, suggesting that income disparity was a stronger determining factor than race.[27]

Despite the controversy surrounding their political strategy, BLM organizers viewed it as a way to hold leaders accountable for representing their interests. "Every successful social movement in this country's history has used disruption as a strategy to fight for social change. Whether it was the Boston Tea Party to the sit-ins at lunch counters throughout the South, no change has been won without disruptive action,"[28] Garza stated. "If we're not making decisions about policy and about representation, if we are not creating our own independent, progressive political force to counter what is a potent backlash to our very existence, we'll be gone,"[29] she added.

Condemnation Following Police Shootings

The BLM movement came under increased public scrutiny in July 2016, following ambush-style attacks on police officers in Dallas, Texas, and Baton Rouge, Louisiana. The shootings occurred in the midst of BLM protests over the police-involved deaths of two black men, Alton Sterling and Philando Castile. Sterling was arrested on July 6 for selling CDs illegally on the street. He was shot five times in the chest at close range while he was being restrained on the ground by Baton Rouge police officers, who claimed they thought he was reaching for a weapon. A witness captured the incident on video. One day later, Castile was shot and killed by a police officer during a routine traffic stop in St. Paul, Minnesota. Castile informed the officer that he had a registered gun in his vehicle, and the officer shot him as he reached for his wallet in response to a request for identification. Castile's girlfriend streamed the fatal encounter on Facebook Live, where it was viewed more than 5 million times. The BLM network organized peaceful demonstrations in dozens of cities across the country to express outrage over these incidents.

During a protest march in Dallas on July 7, however, a sniper killed five police officers. The shooter said his motive was retaliation for the recent shootings of black men by white police officers. Ten days later, a gunman described as a "black separatist" killed three police officers and injured three others in a purported revenge shooting in Baton Rouge. BLM leaders condemned both of the shootings and noted that neither gunman was associated with the movement. Nevertheless, the intentional targeting of police officers sent shockwaves through the United States and generated intense criticism of the BLM movement.

Commentators on the political right claimed that BLM's antipolice rhetoric and protests created an atmosphere that imperiled the lives of law enforcement officers. They pointed to studies suggesting that increasing levels of public scrutiny and hostility after Ferguson had made police officers more reluctant to stop people for minor offenses or to use appropriate force when necessary. This theory, known as the Ferguson effect, claimed that less proactive policing had emboldened criminals and led to higher rates of violent crime. "Law and order are breaking down in inner cities; officers are surrounded by hostile, jeering crowds when they get out of their squad cars to conduct an investigation," wrote Heather Mac Donald, a leading proponent of the Ferguson effect. "Resistance to arrest is up, increasing the chances of an officer's own use of force. And race riots are returning to American cities. The current mendacious narrative about policing and race has to change or we can expect to see further violent-crime increases and further racial violence."[30]

Some BLM critics contended that racial profiling in law enforcement was justified because African Americans were far more likely to commit violent crimes than people of other races. Mac Donald cited statistics for Chicago indicating that blacks committed 76 percent of all homicides while comprising only 35 percent of the city's population. In comparison, whites committed 4 percent of all homicides while comprising 28 percent of the city's population, and Hispanics committed 19 percent of homicides while comprising 30 percent of the population.[31] BLM leaders denied the existence of a Ferguson effect. They argued that police became less aggressive not because they felt under siege, but because BLM protests made them more sensitive to public concerns about racial profiling and excessive force. They portrayed the shift in police tactics as a positive development that addressed the long-standing problem of overpolicing in black communities. They also asserted that violent crime rates were influenced by many factors other than race, including government policies and socioeconomic conditions.

Some critics on the political right vilified the Black Lives Matter movement, describing BLM as a hate group or a terrorist organization. A controversial online advertisement for the National Rifle Association claimed that BLM protesters "smash windows, burn cars, shut down interstates and airports, bully and terrorize the law-abiding—until the only option left is for the police to do their jobs and stop the madness. And when that happens, they'll use it as an excuse for their outrage."[32] The Southern Poverty Law Center (SPLC), a civil rights organization that tracks hate groups in the United States, objected to the characterization of BLM as a hate group. "Black Lives Matter is not a racist group; anyone can join. It's a movement to expand civil rights for the oppressed in this society. It's a peaceful protest against oppression," said Heidi Beirich of SPLC. "There's simply no equivalence between Black Lives Matter and a hate group. It's truly offensive to equate them."[33] Some opponents appeared to advocate violence against BLM activists and their supporters. "This is now war," Joe Walsh, a conservative talk show host and former Republican congressman from Illinois, tweeted following the Dallas shootings. "Watch out Obama. Watch out Black Lives Matter punks. Real America is coming for you."[34]

Confrontations with White Nationalists and the Alt-Right

After Trump assumed the presidency in 2017, white supremacist and white nationalist groups became more visible and active in the United States. Various explanations have been offered for this phenomenon, including assertions that Trump's own rhetoric encouraged racists to come out of the shadows. Observers also attributed the surge in openly racist speech, symbols, and practices to an increasingly virulent "alt-right" backlash against the BLM movement.

A violent clash occurred between white nationalists and counterprotesters from BLM and other progressive groups in Charlottesville,

Virginia, in August 2017. Hundreds of white nationalists, Ku Klux Klan (KKK) members, and neo-Nazis gathered for a Unite the Right rally to protest the removal of a statue of Confederate General Robert E. Lee from a city park. Many of the marchers carried torches, Confederate flags, Trump campaign signs, or banners bearing swastikas, and they shouted racial, ethnic, and misogynistic insults. Some wore helmets and carried weapons. The Charlottesville BLM chapter tried to convince city officials to prohibit the rally, and when that effort failed, they organized a nonviolent counter-protest. Local and state police could not keep the alt-right marchers separated from the counter-protesters, however, and a series of brawls ensued. In the midst of the chaos, a white supremacist drove a vehicle into a crowd of counter-protesters, killing one person and injuring more than a dozen others.

Trump waited 48 hours to comment on the events in Charlottesville, and his initial remarks did not denounce white supremacy. Instead, he made an equivocal statement condemning the "egregious display of hatred, bigotry, and violence, on many sides. On many sides." In a follow-up statement, Trump defended the alt-right protesters further by claiming that there were "very fine people on both sides"[35] of the clash in Charlottesville. "I think there is blame on both sides," he added in a press conference. "You had a group on one side that was bad and you had a group on the other side that was also very violent. Nobody wants to say it, but I will say it right now."[36] KKK leader David Duke expressed his appreciation for Trump's stance, which he interpreted as a rebuke of BLM and other counter-protesters. "Thank you President Trump for your honesty and courage to tell the truth about #Charlottesville and condemn the leftist terrorists in BLM,"[37] he tweeted.

Trump came under intense criticism from leaders of both political parties for appearing sympathetic to white nationalist views and implying moral equivalency between white supremacists and those who demonstrated against their racist beliefs and practices. They accused the president of normalizing bigotry and legitimizing intolerance and hatred. "From the beginning, President Trump has sheltered and encouraged the forces of bigotry and discrimination," said Democratic House Minority Leader Nancy Pelosi. "There is only one side to be on when a white supremacist mob brutalizes and murders in America." Republican Speaker of the House Paul Ryan added, "We must be clear. White supremacy is repulsive. This bigotry is counter to all this country stands for. There can be no moral ambiguity."[38]

BLM supporters viewed Charlottesville and Trump's response to it as proof that their demands for social justice had generated a racist backlash. "Charlottesville was and shall remain a chilling reminder of the entrenched racism against black people and other marginalized groups in the U.S.," Yolanda Moses wrote in the *Conversation*. "Rather than embracing diversity and inclusion, the people who marched focused their anger on the apparent need to take back their country and 'make it great again.' This means taking the country back for white people who want to make it theirs and only theirs 'again.' It is not an inclusive or socially just sentiment."[39] Some supporters argued that the BLM movement arose in response to white supremacy, which was always present in American society but became more visible under Trump. "In white-dominated societies, nearly any demand for equality by people of color is met by a backlash couched in terms of white victimhood. This has been as true for Black Lives Matter as it was for the civil rights movement," Smith wrote in the *Conversation*. "The anger harnessed by figures like Donald Trump and Rudy Giuliani is the anger of white privilege forced to defend itself."[40]

Some commentators on the political right continued to equate BLM with alt-right groups, describing black activists as violent extremists who advocated antiwhite racism. In August 2017, the FBI released an intelligence assessment entitled, "Black Identity Extremists Likely Motivated to Target Law Enforcement Officers." BLM activists argued that the report was politically motivated to distract from alt-right extremism. They objected to the term "black identity extremists," which they said could be misconstrued to apply to peaceful BLM protesters as well as anyone who felt pride in their African heritage. BLM leaders also emphasized their belief that improving black lives would improve the nation as a whole. "White people tend to see racism as a zero-sum game, meaning that gains for African Americans come at their expense," wrote Richard Cohen, president of SPLC. "Black people see it differently. From their point of view, the rights pie can get bigger for everyone."[41]

Notes

1. "On Views of Race and Inequality, Blacks and Whites Are Worlds Apart," Pew Research Center, June 27, 2016, http://www.pewsocialtrends.org/files/2016/06/ST_2016.06.27_Race-Inequality-Final.pdf.
2. Melina Abdullah, "Black Lives Matter Is a Revolutionary Peace Movement," *Conversation*, October 11, 2017, https://theconversation.com/black-lives-matter-is-a-revolutionary-peace-movement-85449.
3. *2 Fists Up* (documentary film), Spike Lee's Lil' Joints, 2016, https://www.youtube.com/watch?v=3eW-31F_7mY.
4. David Smith, "The Backlash against Black Lives Matter Is Just More Evidence of Injustice," *Conversation*, October 31, 2017, https://theconversation.com/the-backlash-against-black-lives-matter-is-just-more-evidence-of-injustice-85587.
5. Julia Craven, "Black Lives Matter Co-Founder Wants to Live in a World Where All Lives Matter," *Huffington Post*, June 20, 2016, https://www.huffingtonpost.com/entry/alicia-garza-black-lives-matter_us_5767fb71e4b015db1bc9dbd8.
6. Brendan Bordelon, " 'Blood on His Hands': A Phalanx of NYPD Officers Turn Backs on de Blasio at Press Conference," *National Review*, December 20, 2014, http://www.nationalreview.com/corner/410708.
7. Ciara McCarthy, "More U.S. Police Officers Killed in 2016—But Number Still Below Ten-Year Average," *Guardian*, December 29, 2016, https://www.theguardian.com/us-news/2016/dec/29/police-killed-2016-average.
8. Jamilah Lemieux, "NYPD Blues: The Anti-Police Brutality Movement Didn't Kill Any Cops," *Ebony*, December 22, 2014, http://www.ebony.com/news-views/nypd-blues-the-anti-police-brutality-movement-didnt-kill-any-cops-405#axzz55EomGkre.
9. Julia Craven, "33 Blue Lives Matter Bills Have Been Introduced across 14 States This Year," *Huffington Post*, December 12, 2017, http://www.huffingtonpost.com.au/entry/blue-black-lives-matter-police-bills-states_us_58b61488e4b0780bac2e31b8.
10. Dawn Ennis, "Black Lives Matter Labels Trump a 'Terrorist' and a 'Fascist,' " *LGBTQ Nation*, July 22, 2016, https://www.lgbtqnation.com/2016/07/black-lives-matter-labels-donald-trump-terrorist-fascist/.
11. "Oprah Winfrey's Comments about Recent Protests and Ferguson Spark Controversy," *People*, January 1, 2015, http://people.com/celebrity/oprah-on-recent-protests-and-ferguson/.
12. Radley Balko, "The Black Lives Matter Policy Agenda Is Practical, Thoughtful—And Urgent," *Washington Post*, August 25, 2015, https://www.washingtonpost.com/news/the-watch/wp/2015/08/25/the-black-lives-matter-policy-agenda-is-practical-thoughtful-and-urgent/?utm_term=.d55c8b795cf7.

13. Mukul Devichand, "Will Black Lives Matter Change America in an Election Year?" BBC News, January 30, 2016, http://www.bbc.com/news/blogs-trending-35444899.

14. Brittney Cooper, "Eleven Major Misconceptions about the Black Lives Matter Movement," *Cosmopolitan*, September 8, 2015, http://www.cosmopolitan.com/politics/a45930/misconceptions-black-lives-matter-movement/.

15. Barbara Reynolds, "I Was a Civil Rights Activist in the 1960s. But It's Hard for Me to Get behind Black Lives Matter," *Washington Post*, August 25, 2015, https://www.washingtonpost.com/posteverything/wp/2015/08/24/i-was-a-civil-rights-activist-in-the-1960s-but-its-hard-for-me-to-get-behind-black-lives-matter/?tid=a_inl&utm_term=.0788f0300ddd.

16. Hillary Crosley Coker, "Activist Johnetta Elzie Talks Ferguson and Black Lives Matter," *Jezebel*, July 17, 2015, https://jezebel.com/activist-johnetta-elzie-talks-ferguson-black-lives-ma-1718374170.

17. Elahe Izadi, "Black Lives Matter and America's Long History of Resisting Civil Rights Protesters," *Washington Post*, April 19, 2016, https://www.washingtonpost.com/news/the-fix/wp/2016/04/19/black-lives-matters-and-americas-long-history-of-resisting-civil-rights-protesters/?utm_term=.f5f4fde93ff6.

18. John Blake, "Is Black Lives Matter Blowing It?" CNN, August 2, 2016, https://www.cnn.com/2016/07/29/us/black-lives-matter-blowing-it/index.html.

19. Aaron Randle, "Now You See Me: A Look at the World of Activist Johnetta Elzie," *Complex*, March 8, 2016, http://www.complex.com/life/2016/03/johnetta-elzie-profile.

20. Craven, "Black Lives Matter Co-Founder Wants to Live in a World Where All Lives Matter."

21. Evan Halper and Kurtis Lee, "How Black Lives Matter Forced Campaigns to Toss Their Strategies on Black Voters," *Los Angeles Times*, July 31, 2015, http://www.latimes.com/nation/la-na-campaign-black-lives-20150731-story.html.

22. Jay Caspian Kang, "Our Demand Is Simple: Stop Killing Us," *New York Times*, May 4, 2015, https://www.nytimes.com/2015/05/10/magazine/our-demand-is-simple-stop-killing-us.html.

23. David Weigel, "Three Words Republicans That Wrestle With: 'Black Lives Matter'," *Washington Post*, July 12, 2016, https://www.washingtonpost.com/politics/three-words-that-republicans-wrestle-with-black-lives-matter/2016/07/12/f5a9dfdc-4878-11e6-90a8-fb84201e0645_story.html?utm_term=.ce44684e54f9.

24. Ibid.

25. Jose A. DelReal, "'Get 'em Out!' Racial Tensions Explode at Donald Trump's Rallies," *Washington Post*, March 12, 2016, https://www.washingtonpost.com/politics/get-him-out-racial-tensions-explode-at-donald-trumps-rallies/2016/03/11/b9764884-e6ee-11e5-bc08-3e03a5b41910_story.html?utm_term=.28be3c43f15f.

26. Ibid.
27. Michael Harriot, "Why We Never Talk about Black-on-Black Crime," *Root*, October 3, 2017, https://www.theroot.com/why-we-never-talk-about-black -on-black-crime-an-answer-1819092337.
28. Craven, "Black Lives Matter Co-Founder Wants to Live in a World Where All Lives Matter."
29. Nathalie Baptiste, "Origins of a Movement," *Nation*, February 9, 2017, https:// www.thenation.com/article/origins-of-a-movement/.
30. Heather Mac Donald, "Hillary's Debate Lies," *City Journal*, September 27, 2016, https://www.city-journal.org/html/hillarys-debate-lies-14759.html.
31. Aaron Bandler, "Seven Statistics You Need to Know about Black-on-Black Crime," *Daily Wire*, July 13, 2016, https://www.dailywire.com/news/7441/ 7-statistics-you-need-know-about-black-black-crime-aaron-bandler.
32. Natasha Bertrand, "A Chilling National Rifle Association Ad Gaining Traction Online Appears to Be 'An Open Call to Violence,'" *Business Insider*, June 29, 2017, http://www.businessinsider.com/national-rifle-association-ad -call-to-violence-2017-6.
33. Touré, "A Year Inside the Black Lives Matter Movement," *Rolling Stone*, December 7, 2017, https://www.rollingstone.com/politics/news/toure-inside -black-lives-matter-w513190.
34. Tom LoBianco and Olivia Beavers, "Ex-Rep. Joe Walsh Defends Tweet Threatening 'War' on Obama," CNN, July 9, 2016, https://www.cnn.com /2016/07/08/politics/joe-walsh-obama-war-tweet/index.html.
35. Glenn Thrush and Maggie Haberman, "Trump Gives White Supremacists an Unequivocal Boost," *New York Times*, August 15, 2017, https://www.nytimes.com /2017/08/15/us/politics/trump-charlottesville-white-nationalists.html? mcubz=0&mtrref=en.wikipedia.org&gwh=0E2E214849F4FEC10AA800B67A 4B1E90&gwt=pay.
36. Andrew Rafferty, Marianna Sotomayor, and Daniel Arkin, "Trump Says 'Two Sides' Share Blame for Charlottesville Rally Violence," NBC News, August 16, 2017, https://www.nbcnews.com/news/us-news/trump-defends-all-sides -comment-n793001.
37. Ibid.
38. Ibid.
39. Yolanda Moses, "We Cannot Deny the Violence of White Supremacy Anymore," *Conversation*, October 25, 2017, https://theconversation.com/ we-cannot-deny-the-violence-of-white-supremacy-any-more-86139.
40. Smith, "The Backlash against Black Lives Matter Is Just More Evidence of Injustice."
41. Richard Cohen, "Black Lives Matter Is Not a Hate Group," Southern Poverty Law Center, July 19, 2016, https://www.splcenter.org/news/2016/07/19/black -lives-matter-not-hate-group.

CHAPTER SEVEN

Racial Injustice in
America

Between the Ferguson protests in 2014 and the inauguration of
President Donald Trump in January 2017, the Black Lives Matter
(BLM) movement accumulated a substantial list of achievements.
President Barack Obama convened a task force to develop recommendations toward improving the relationship between law enforcement
officers and the communities they serve. The U.S. Department of
Justice (DOJ) provided racial bias training to 28,000 federal employees. Police departments in dozens of cities reviewed their policies
regarding the use of force and introduced changes aimed at protecting
the rights of citizens, such as requiring officers to wear body cameras.
Democratic presidential candidates acknowledged racial injustice as
an important campaign issue and proposed policies to address it. Residents of Chicago, Cleveland, and several other cities voted local prosecutors out of office for failing to investigate police violence
aggressively.

Despite these successes, however, many BLM activists feel that
their work is just beginning. They view criminal justice reform as the
first stage in a larger, ongoing struggle against structural racism and
inequality that undervalues black lives in American society. "People
think, 'Well, you had the civil rights movement, and now black people

are equal, so what are you complaining about?'" noted BLM cofounder Alicia Garza. "It's important that we really talk about how that is a stage in an unfinished project that really has been going on for hundreds of years."[1]

As the BLM movement has matured, organizers have expanded beyond protests and into the realm of policy. The BLM movement has increasingly targeted broad, systemic factors that hinder the progress of black citizens and communities, such as racial disparities in income, employment, housing, health, and education. "Activism looks like a lot of different things: It can look like voting, it can look like protest, it can look like calling your representatives," said Aditi Juneja, a member of Campaign Zero. "The question shouldn't be 'Will this activism be sustained?' because for many people the work is very personal, and it isn't going to stop. The question is how it will sustain and how it will continue to manifest."[2]

Socioeconomic Inequality

According to a Pew Research Center survey released in 2016, white Americans are evenly split about the state of race relations in the United States, with 46 percent describing them as generally good and 45 percent saying they were generally bad. Black Americans express a more pessimistic view, however, with 61 percent of respondents describing race relations as bad and only 34 percent calling them good.[3] On the surface, there are many indications that the country has made progress toward racial equality—the most obvious being Obama's 2008 election as the nation's first black president. Yet BLM activists reject the notion that the United States has entered a postracial era in which all Americans enjoy equal opportunity. Instead, they point to statistics showing that black communities continue to lag behind white communities in a number of key socioeconomic measures, and they argue that systemic racism is the main factor responsible.

Income levels and employment rates are significantly different for black and white Americans. As of 2014, according to the Pew Research Center, median household income in the United States was $71,300 for white families and $43,300 for black families. The income disparity remains consistent even at higher education levels, suggesting that a college degree is not enough to level the playing field for African Americans. In households where the head of the family is college educated, the median annual income was $106,600 for white families and $82,300 for black families. White Americans have an even bigger advantage in terms of median household net worth, with the $144,200 value of white households 13 times higher than the $11,200 value of black households. The stark difference in this key measure of financial stability is largely explained by racial disparity in rates of homeownership. Only 43 percent of black families own a home, compared to 72 percent of white families.[4]

In 2015, the unemployment rate for blacks, at 10.3 percent, was more than double that of whites, at 4.5 percent. Partly as a result, 26 percent of black people lived in poverty, compared to 10 percent of white people. High-poverty neighborhoods typically exhibit higher levels of environmental pollution, drug addiction, gang activity, and violent crime. A 2016 study by the Kaiser Family Foundation found that black Americans fared worse than white Americans on 24 out of 29 measures of health status and outcomes. Black people were less likely to have health insurance and access to quality health care, for instance, and more likely to experience various health issues, including obesity, diabetes, heart disease, and HIV infection. The teen birth rate among African Americans, at 34.7 per 1,000 population, was nearly twice as high as among white Americans, at 17.2 per 1,000.[5] As a result, 71 percent of black children were born outside of marriage in 2014, compared to 29 percent of white children, and black children were three times more likely than white children to be raised by single parent.[6]

The reasons behind the socioeconomic disadvantages experienced by African Americans have long been a subject of intense debate. During the civil rights movement of the 1960s, protesters succeeded in convincing influential political leaders that institutional racism presented a major barrier to equality. In 1967, for instance, President Lyndon Johnson convened the National Advisory Commission on Civil Disorders (commonly known as the Kerner Commission) to investigate the causes of racial unrest in Detroit, Chicago, Los Angeles, and other large cities. The commission's report, released the following year, placed the blame squarely on systemic racism and failed policies that kept black citizens segregated in substandard housing and offered them limited economic opportunities. "Our nation is moving toward two societies—one black and one white—separate and unequal,"[7] it famously concluded.

The recommendations made by the Kerner Commission were largely ignored, however, and many of the problems that the report identified continue to impact black communities in the United States 50 years later. The popular understanding of the root cause of those problems has shifted significantly during that time, however, especially among white Americans. The 2016 Pew Research Center survey found that 70 percent of black respondents, but only 36 percent of white respondents, believe racial discrimination is a major barrier preventing blacks from getting ahead in the United States. White respondents instead tend to attribute the problems facing black communities to deficiencies within those communities, such as family instability or a lack of role models. "Since the Kerner Commission's admission, there has been a complete reversal in the dominant notions of who is to blame for persistent black poverty, unemployment, and incarceration," wrote Khury Petersen-Smith in *ISR*. "An ideological component of the rollback of the civil rights and Black Power movements has been the widespread dissemination and acceptance of the notion that failure to succeed in U.S. society is the result of the shortcomings of black people. The idea that black people simply need to 'try harder' is voiced by prominent individuals ranging from conservative media pundits to prominent black figures like Bill Cosby and President Obama."[8]

School Segregation and the Achievement Gap

One of the key areas of concern for black activists seeking to close the socioeconomic gap between black and white families in America is education. The 1954 U.S. Supreme Court ruling in *Brown v. Board of Education*, which outlawed racial segregation in the nation's public schools, was the first victory in the civil rights movement. Yet upholding the promise of equal educational opportunity for students of color remains a challenge for the BLM movement six decades later. Statistics have shown that public schools in the United States have become increasingly segregated since 1988, when nearly half of all black children attended a racially integrated school. As of 2013, researchers from the University of California at Los Angeles found that 37 percent of schools nationwide were intensely segregated, meaning that more than 90 percent of students were of the same race. The percentage of intensely segregated nonwhite schools more than tripled between 1988 and 2013, from 5.7 percent to 18.6 percent. School segregation was most pronounced in the state of New York, where two-thirds of black students attended a school where the enrollment was less than 10 percent white.[9]

American public schools have also grown more segregated by class. From 2000 to 2014, according to the U.S. Government Accountability Office, the number of schools that were segregated by both poverty and race more than doubled, from 7,009 to 15,089.[10] In 1993, a typical black student attended a school in which 37 percent of fellow students had family income low enough to meet federal standards for free or subsidized lunch. Twenty years later, a typical black student attended a school comprised 68 percent low-income students.[11] "While segregation as it is practiced today may be different than it was sixty years ago, it is no less pernicious," wrote Nikole Hannah-Jones of ProPublica. "It involves the removal and isolation of poor black and Latino students, in particular, from everyone else.... Nationally, the achievement gap between black and white students, which greatly narrowed during the era in which schools grew more integrated, widened as they became less so."[12]

The trend toward resegregation can be attributed partly to a series of court decisions that have rolled back federal monitoring and enforcement of desegregation efforts. In 1991, for instance, the U.S. Supreme Court ruled in *Oklahoma City v. Dowell* that school districts could be released from court-ordered integration plans once they had demonstrated earnest compliance, even if it resulted in future segregation. The increasing prevalence of school-choice programs and charter schools is another factor that has contributed to the trend. Beginning with *Brown v. Board of Education*, however, research has consistently shown that racial segregation creates educational challenges for black students and perpetuates inequality in education.

Although high school completion rates were similar for black students and white students in 2013, the National Assessment for Educational Progress (NAEP) revealed a major gap in academic achievement. The average black high school senior placed in the 19th percentile in math and in the 22nd percentile for reading, meaning that 81 percent of white high school seniors scored higher in math and 78 percent scored higher in reading.[13] Some analysts blame the disparity on school segregation, which tends to give black students unequal access to educational resources.

A 2012 report by the Center for American Progress noted that intensely segregated white schools spent an average of $733 more per pupil than intensely segregated nonwhite schools. In addition, the study found a strong correlation between segregation and school spending: per-pupil funding decreased by $75 for every 10 percent increase in students of color. In California, schools with more than 90 percent nonwhite students received $4,380 less per pupil than schools with more than 90 percent white students. For an average-sized school, the difference in funding amounts to $3.3 million per year.[14]

Education advocates argue that this amount would enable a pre-dominantly nonwhite school to hire additional classroom teachers, upgrade facilities, purchase computers and other technology, and offer more college-preparatory courses and enrichment opportunities, such as music and art programs. By reducing the quality of education available to nonwhite students, the lack of funding makes them less likely to go to college. Only 23 percent of black students pursued higher education in 2015, compared to 36 percent of white students.[15] The school integration that took place from *Brown v. Board* through the 1980s "fundamentally enhanced the quality of education received by students of all races," according to law professor Derek Black. "But through a combination of willful, blind, and benign neglect, nearly all of those gains have been lost."[16]

Incarceration and the "Cradle-to-Prison Pipeline"

As of 2015, the United States had the highest rate of incarceration in the world at nearly 700 prisoners per 100,000 population (although the archipelago nation of Seychelles technically had a higher rate, with nearly 800 people in prison, its total population was less than 100,000). By comparison, the average rate of incarceration for all countries worldwide was 144 per 100,000 population. The total U.S. prison population of 2.2 million people was larger than that of any other nation and accounted for nearly one-fourth of the global total.[17]

Racial and ethnic minorities comprise a disproportionate share of those incarcerated in the United States. According to the National Association for the Advancement of Colored People (NAACP), African Americans and Hispanics accounted for 56 percent of all people in jail or prison in 2015, even though together they made up only 32 percent of the overall population.[18] The incarceration rate for black people, at 1,408 per 100,000 population, was more than five times higher than that of whites (at 275 per 100,000) and nearly four times higher than that of Hispanics (at 378). Of the 1.3 million people held in state prisons, 38 percent were black, compared to 35 percent white and 21 percent Hispanic. In a dozen states, the majority of prisoners were black.[19]

BLM activists attribute the racial disparities in incarceration rates to institutional racism in the American criminal justice system. They argue that legislation, court fines, sentencing policies, police practices, and socioeconomic inequality all contribute to the criminalization of black people and the overpolicing of black communities. A frequently cited example is the law enforcement strategy known as "broken-windows policing." Based on a theory developed in the 1980s, it centers around the idea that issuing citations for minor offenses, and rewarding police officers for doing so, helps maintain order and prevent more serious crime. The strategy was implemented in New York City and several other large municipalities, and proponents noted that violent crime rates declined in some cases. Studies did not find a causal link, however, and critics charge that broken-windows policing often has unintended negative consequences for low-income and minority populations. They argue that the strategy encourages police to use aggressive tactics in response to trivial misbehavior, such as when Eric Garner was placed in a choke hold for selling loose cigarettes on a Staten Island street. They also claim that it damages the relationship between police officers and the communities they serve, creates an atmosphere of mistrust that reduces public cooperation, imposes burdensome fines on poor people for minor offenses, places a strain on court systems, and contributes to the problem of mass incarceration.[20]

BLM activists contend that the federal government's "war on drugs" also has a disproportionate impact on African Americans. Since policies like zero tolerance, mandatory minimum sentencing, and "three strikes" for habitual offenders were introduced, the number of people incarcerated in U.S. prisons for drug offenses has increased by more than 1,000 percent, from 40,900 in 1980 to 469,545 in 2015.[21] Although white Americans are more likely to use cocaine, marijuana, methamphetamines, and several other types of illegal drugs, black Americans are three times more likely to be arrested for drug offenses.[22] As a result, half of all inmates held in state prisons and local jails for drug offenses in 2015 were black. Once incarcerated, black men serve terms that are more than 20 times longer, on average, than white men serve for the same offense.[23] Incarceration compounds the issue of poverty by increasing the number of single-parent families and limiting employment opportunities for ex-convicts once they are released.

Civil rights advocates coined the term "cradle-to-prison pipeline" to describe the combination of risk factors that increase the likelihood that black youth—and especially black males—will end up in the criminal justice system. Black children are more likely than white children to be born to teenage mothers, to be raised in single-parent households, and to live in poverty. They are also more likely to face educational disadvantages in poorly funded, segregated schools. Black children are nearly nine times more likely than white children to have an incarcerated parent, which increases the risk that they will be incarcerated. Black children also face racial bias in school discipline, policing, and sentencing. As a result, studies have shown that one out of every three black boys born in 2001 will end up in prison at some point in his life. "Incarceration is becoming the new American apartheid and poor children of color are the fodder," wrote activist Marian Wright Edelman. "It is time to sound a loud alarm about this threat to American unity and community, act to stop the growing criminalization of children at younger and younger ages, and tackle the unjust treatment of minority youths and adults in the juvenile and adult criminal justice systems with urgency and persistence."[24]

Suppression of Black Voting Rights

Ever since African American men gained the right to vote in 1870 with the ratification of the Fifteenth Amendment, various states have enacted measures to restrict or suppress black voting rights. Although many of these discriminatory measures were prohibited by the Voting Rights Act of 1965, which was the culminating legislative achievement of the civil rights movement, the Supreme Court weakened the landmark law in 2013. In *Shelby County v. Holder*, the justices voted 5–4 to invalidate the preclearance provision, which had required states and municipalities with a history of discrimination against minority voters to obtain federal approval before changing their voting rules. Citing the strong minority support that helped Obama become the first black president, the Court claimed that the nation had overcome the problem of racial discrimination in voting, so the provision was no longer necessary. Fourteen states—including five that previously had been subjected to federal preclearance under the Voting Rights Act—responded to the ruling by passing new restrictions on voting prior to the 2016 election.

Many of the new voting rules and procedures were ostensibly aimed at curbing voting fraud. Conservative lawmakers have often expressed concern about illegal voting, claiming that it is a major problem nationwide and contributed to Obama's victories. The overwhelming evidence, however, does not support these claims. A 2012 study by researchers at Arizona State University found only 10 cases of voter impersonation over the previous dozen years, or one case for every 15 million registered voters in the United States,[25] while a 2016 study by researchers at Dartmouth University uncovered no evidence of voting fraud in that year's elections.[26] Voting rights advocates charge that illegal voting is a myth used to justify restrictions that discriminate against minority voters, who tend to favor Democratic Party candidates.

Voter ID laws were among the most popular new measures introduced by Republican-controlled state legislatures. These laws require voters to produce specific types of photo identification at polling places, such as a driver's license or state-issued ID card. Although proponents claim voter ID laws are a straightforward way to prevent voter impersonation, critics argue that the requirements create barriers to voting that disproportionately impact certain groups of citizens, such as students, the elderly, low-income people, and racial and ethnic minorities. A study of voter ID laws in the state of Indiana, for instance, found that black citizens were 11.5 percent less likely than white citizens to have the forms of identification required for voting.[27] In 2016, a federal judge overturned a Texas voter ID law, ruling that "racial discrimination was a motivating factor" in its passage.[28]

Other actions taken by states that often had the effect of disenfranchising black voters include reducing early voting opportunities, closing polling places, and purging voter registration lists. According to research conducted by the Leadership Conference Education Fund, jurisdictions that were subject to preclearance prior to 2013 operated 868 fewer polling locations in 2016 than they did when they were covered by the Voting Rights Act.[29] Restrictions on early voting and reductions in the number of polling places decrease black voter turnout by causing long lines. Low-income and minority voters are disproportionately affected by extended wait times because they are less likely to have flexible work hours, child care options, and reliable access to transportation.

Most jurisdictions conduct regular reviews of voter registration records and remove the names of people who have died, moved away, or failed to vote in multiple elections. In many cases, however, purges of voter rolls have been done in ways that unfairly target people of color. In 2016, for instance, Georgia took steps to remove 35,000 voters from its rolls on the basis of minor discrepancies in registration records, such as a missing hyphen or transposed number. The state was forced to put its plans on hold, however, when it was revealed that black voters accounted for 64 percent of those impacted by the purge.[30] Since African Americans only make up 32 percent of Georgia's population, they were eight times more likely to be purged from the rolls than white voters.

Felon disenfranchisement laws have also disproportionately suppressed black voting rights in the United States. As of 2014, all but two states prohibited people from voting while they were incarcerated for a felony offense, while 31 states prohibited people from voting while they were on parole or probation. Four states banned ex-felons from voting even after they had completed all the terms of their sentences, and many other states imposed rigorous conditions for restoring voting rights to former offenders. Given the high rates of incarceration among African Americans, these laws mean that 2.2 million black adults, 7.7 percent of black people of voting age, are not allowed to cast ballots.[31]

Another method used to limit black political power is partisan redistricting or gerrymandering, a process in which state legislatures redraw congressional district boundaries in ways that favor the interests of one political party or candidate. Although both political parties engage in gerrymandering, Republican lawmakers are more likely to employ the practice to the disadvantage of minority voters, due to their historic tendency to support Democratic candidates. In North Carolina, for instance, Republican state legislators packed large numbers of black voters into a few districts and diluted their voting strength in others. In 2017, the Supreme Court struck down the plan as an unconstitutional racial gerrymander and ordered North Carolina to redraw its legislative district map.[32]

Notes

1. Heather Smith, "Meet the BART-Stopping Woman behind 'Black Lives Matter,'" *Grist*, December 4, 2014, http://grist.org/politics/stopping-a-bart -train-in-michael-browns-name/.
2. Janell Ross and Wesley Lowery, "Black Lives Matter Shifts from Protests to Policy under Trump," *Chicago Tribune*, May 4, 2017, http://www.chicagotribune.com/ news/nationworld/ct-black-lives-matter-trump-20170504-story.html.
3. "On Views of Race and Inequality, Blacks and Whites Are Worlds Apart," Pew Research Center, June 27, 2016, http://www.pewsocialtrends.org/files/2016/ 06/ST_2016.06.27_Race-Inequality-Final.pdf.
4. Ibid.
5. Samantha Artiga, Julia Foutz, Elizabeth Cornachione, and Rachel Garfield, "Key Facts on Health and Health Care by Race and Ethnicity," Kaiser Family Foundation, June 7, 2016, https://www.kff.org/report-section/key-facts-on -health-and-health-care-by-race-and-ethnicity-section-3-health-status-and -outcomes/.
6. "On Views of Race and Inequality, Blacks and Whites Are Worlds Apart."
7. *Report of the National Advisory Commission on Civil Disorders* (Washington, DC, 1968), 1, https://www.ncjrs.gov/pdffiles1/Digitization/8073NCJRS.pdf.
8. Khury Petersen-Smith, "Black Lives Matter: A New Movement Takes Shape," *International Socialist Review*, no. 96 (Spring 2015), https://isreview.org/issue/ 96/black-lives-matter.
9. Gary Orfield, Jongyeon Ee, Erica Frankenberg, and Genevieve Siegel-Hawley, "Brown at 62: Segregation by Race, Poverty, and State," Civil Rights Project, UCLA, May 16, 2016, https://www.civilrightsproject.ucla.edu/research/k-12 -education/integration-and-diversity/brown-at-62-school-segregation-by -race-poverty-and-state/Brown-at-62-final-corrected-2.pdf.
10. Alexander Nazaryan, "Whites Only: School Segregation Is Back, from Birming- ham to San Francisco," *Newsweek*, May 2, 2017, http://www.newsweek.com/ race-schools-592637.

11. Orfield et al., "Brown at 62: Segregation by Race, Poverty, and State."
12. Nikole Hannah-Jones, "Segregation Now," ProPublica, April 16, 2014, https://www.propublica.org/article/segregation-now-full-text.
13. Lauren Camera, "Achievement Gap between White and Black Students Still Gaping," *U.S. News and World Report*, January 13, 2016, https://www.usnews.com/news/blogs/data-mine/2016/01/13/achievement-gap-between-white-and-black-students-still-gaping.
14. "Students of Color Still Receiving Unequal Education," Center for American Progress, August 22, 2012, https://www.americanprogress.org/issues/education-k-12/news/2012/08/22/32862/students-of-color-still-receiving-unequal-education/.
15. "On Views of Race and Inequality, Blacks and Whites Are Worlds Apart."
16. Dexter Mullins, "Six Decades after Brown Ruling, U.S. Schools Still Segregated," Al Jazeera America, September 25, 2013, http://america.aljazeera.com/articles/2013/9/25/56-years-after-littlerockusschoolssegregatedbyraceandclass.html.
17. Roy Walmsley, "World Prison Population List," 11th ed., World Prison Brief/Institute for Criminal Policy Research, February 2, 2016, http://www.prisonstudies.org/sites/default/files/resources/downloads/world_prison_population_list_11th_edition_0.pdf.
18. "Criminal Justice Fact Sheet," NAACP, 2018, http://www.naacp.org/criminal-justice-fact-sheet/.
19. Ashley Nellis, "The Color of Justice: Racial and Ethnic Disparity in State Prisons," Sentencing Project, 2016, https://www.sentencingproject.org/wp-content/uploads/2016/06/The-Color-of-Justice-Racial-and-Ethnic-Disparity-in-State-Prisons.pdf.
20. Sarah Childress, "The Problem with 'Broken Windows' Policing," PBS *Frontline*, June 28, 2016, https://www.pbs.org/wgbh/frontline/article/the-problem-with-broken-windows-policing/.
21. "Trends in U.S. Corrections," Sentencing Project, 2016, https://sentencingproject.org/wp-content/uploads/2016/01/Trends-in-US-Corrections.pdf.
22. Saki Knafo, "When It Comes to Illegal Drug Use, White America Does the Crime, Black America Gets the Time," *Huffington Post*, September 17, 2013, https://www.huffingtonpost.com/2013/09/17/racial-disparity-drug-use-n_3941346.html.
23. Nellis, "The Color of Justice."
24. Marian Wright Edelman, "The Cradle-to-Prison Pipeline: America's Apartheid," *Huffington Post*, May 25, 2011, https://www.huffingtonpost.com/marian-wright-edelman/the-cradle-to-prison-pipe_b_165163.html.
25. Natasha Khan and Corbin Carson, "Comprehensive Database of Voter Fraud Uncovers No Evidence That Voter ID Is Needed," News 21, August 12, 2012, https://votingrights.news21.com/article/election-fraud/.

26. Rob Wolfe, "Dartmouth Researchers: Fraud Not Shown in 2016 Voting Data," *Valley News*, December 2, 2016, http://www.vnews.com/Dartmouth -Scholars-Study-Claims-Of-Election-Fraud-6647155.

27. Matt A. Barreto, "The Disproportionate Impact of Voter ID Requirements on the Electorate—New Evidence from Indiana," *Political Science*, January 2009, http://mattbarreto.com/papers/PS_VoterID.pdf.

28. *Veasey v. Abbott*, U.S. District Court, Southern District of Texas, April 10, 2017, https://www.brennancenter.org/sites/default/files/legal-work/2017-04 -10_Order_Intent.pdf.

29. Scott Simpson, "The Great Poll Closure," Leadership Conference Education Fund, November 2016, http://civilrightsdocs.info/pdf/reports/2016/poll -closure-report-web.pdf.

30. Liz Kennedy and Danielle Root, "Keeping Voters off Rolls," Center for American Progress, July 18, 2017, https://www.americanprogress.org/issues/ democracy/reports/2017/07/18/435914/keeping-voters-off-rolls/.

31. "Felony Disenfranchisement Laws in the United States," Sentencing Project, April 28, 2014, https://www.sentencingproject.org/publications/felony -disenfranchisement-laws-in-the-united-states/.

32. Vann R. Newkirk II, "The Supreme Court Finds North Carolina's Racial Gerrymandering Unconstitutional," *Atlantic*, May 22, 2017, https://www .theatlantic.com/politics/archive/2017/05/north-carolina-gerrymandering/ 527592/.

Conclusion

The issue that originally galvanized activists to launch the Black Lives Matter (BLM) movement remained relevant four years after its founding. According to the Mapping Police Violence database, 1,147 people were killed by police officers in the United States in 2017. More than half of the people killed by police were either suspected of nonviolent offenses or not suspected of any crime, and at least 149 were unarmed. Black people continued to be disproportionately affected by police violence. African Americans accounted for 27 percent of all people and 37 percent of unarmed people killed by police in 2017. Most instances of police violence went unpunished, as only 13 officers were charged with a crime in relation to a shooting death.[1]

While the BLM movement continues to organize around the issue of criminal justice reform, it also faces significant new challenges following the 2016 presidential election. Many activists are disheartened by Trump's campaign to "Make America Great Again," which they interpret as conveying sympathy toward racist views and antipathy toward BLM's struggle for racial justice. Shortly after Trump's inauguration, the official White House website was updated to include a statement expressing the administration's support for law enforcement and disapproval of BLM protesters. "President Trump will honor our men and women in uniform and will support their mission of protecting the public. The dangerous anti-police atmosphere in America is wrong. The Trump Administration will end it," it read. "Our job is not to make life more comfortable for the rioter, the looter, or the violent disrupter."[2]

A week after Trump's electoral victory, BLM cofounders Alicia Garza, Patrisse Cullors, and Opal Tometi released a public statement reemphasizing their commitment to the cause. "What is true today—and has been true since the seizure of this land—is that when black people and women build power, white people become resentful. Last week, that resentment manifested itself in the election of a white supremacist to the highest office in American government," they wrote. "Donald Trump has promised more death, disenfranchisement, and deportations. We believe him. The violence he will inflict in office, and the permission he gives for others to commit violence, is just beginning to emerge. In the face of this, our commitment remains the same: protect ourselves and our communities."[3]

The Trump administration signaled its intention to roll back some of the gains the BLM movement has made toward criminal justice reform. Under Obama, the U.S. Department of Justice (DOJ) investigated two dozen law enforcement agencies nationwide and entered into oversight agreements with 14 that were found to have demonstrated racial bias. In 2017, however, Attorney General Jeff Sessions directed the Justice Department to review those agreements, which he described as damaging to police morale and public safety. Sessions also outlined administration goals that included cracking down on drug offenses and constructing additional prisons.

Meanwhile, Trump's election has aroused new levels of activism among other groups of citizens who object to the tenor of his campaign or the policies of his administration. New protest movements have emerged to advocate for progressive causes and the rights of women, LGBTQ individuals, immigrants, and low-income families. Some of these movements have adopted the model established by BLM, with trending hashtags on social media followed by organized marches and protests. Some BLM organizers have shifted their strategy to embrace these movements and support their priorities, such as increasing the minimum wage, protecting immigrants from deportation, or standing up for victims of sexual assault. "We are also doing a lot of work to build bridges between other movements and communities caught in the crosshairs of

Trump's agenda," Garza explained. "It's a real opportunity for us to build a movement of movements. . . . Our futures are tied to each other."[4]

Although the new political environment has forced BLM activists to adjust their strategies and tactics, they insist that the movement will continue fighting for both social and legislative change. "I think Black Lives Matter is very relevant today, especially given the rise of white supremacists and white nationalists across, not just this country, but across the globe," said Cullors. "Our work over the last four years has been putting anti-black racism on the map, talking about the impact anti-black racism has on this country, has on local government, has on policy, and how it actually impacts the everyday life of black people."[5]

Garza, whose anguished "Love Letter to Black People" on Facebook launched the movement, encourages supporters to adopt a long-term perspective on the struggle for racial equality. "Do we feel like we're making progress? Yes and no. It is very much two steps forward, one step back," she stated. "And I think that that is why it's important for us to have a long view. The first major piece of civil rights legislation in this country took forty years. *Forty*. . . . So we're doing pretty good."[6]

Notes

1. "2017 Police Violence Report," Mapping Police Violence, 2018, https://policeviolencereport.org/.
2. Dara Lind, "Trump's White House Site Vows to End the 'Anti-Police Atmosphere' in America," *Vox*, January 20, 2017, https://www.vox.com/2017/1/20/14338632/trump-whitehouse-gov-blue-lives-matter.
3. Aaron Morrison, "Black Lives Matter Issues a Statement on Trump's Election," *Mic*, November 15, 2016, https://mic.com/articles/159496/exclusive-black-lives-matter-issues-a-statement-on-trump-s-election#.rVNaYDbxq.
4. Janell Ross and Wesley Lowery, "Black Lives Matter Shifts from Protests to Policy under Trump," *Chicago Tribune*, May 4, 2017, http://www.chicagotribune.com/news/nationworld/ct-black-lives-matter-trump-20170504-story.html.
5. Ann M. Simmons and Jaweed Kaleem, "A Founder of Black Lives Matter Answers a Question on Many Minds: Where Did It Go?" *Los Angeles Times*, August 25, 2017, http://www.latimes.com/nation/la-na-patrisse-cullors-black-lives-matter-2017-htmlstory.html.
6. Elle Hunt, "Alicia Garza on the Beauty and the Burden of Black Lives Matter," *Guardian*, September 2, 2016, https://www.theguardian.com/us-news/2016/sep/02/alicia-garza-on-the-beauty-and-the-burden-of-black-lives-matter.

Biographical Sketches

Michael Brown (1996–2014)

Teenager whose death sparked the Ferguson protests and fueled the growth of the Black Lives Matter movement

Michael Orlandus Darrion Brown, known as Mike Mike to his family, was born on May 20, 1996, in Florissant, Missouri. His parents, Michael Brown and Lezley McSpadden, were teenagers at the time of his birth. After they split up, Mike Mike lived primarily with his mother but remained close to his father. He was raised within a large extended family whose members all lived in the St. Louis suburbs and frequently got together for weekend barbeques.

Brown was a rambunctious child who climbed out of playpens and drew on the walls with his crayons. As he got older, he enjoyed playing video games, especially Call of Duty: Zombies and PlayStation Home. He also liked listening to rap music and was rarely spotted without his headphones. During his teen years, Brown began composing his own rap songs, with lyrics that alternated between sentimental and vulgar. He posted some of his songs on SoundCloud, an online music-sharing site.

By the time he reached the age of 18, Brown had grown to be a large man, standing six feet, four inches tall and weighing nearly 300 pounds. His friends and family described him as a "gentle giant," however, and claimed that he used his intimidating size to avoid physical conflict. According to his mother, he was too timid to play high school football, although classmates and coaches tried to convince him to join the team. Brown tended to be quiet and reserved around strangers, but he often told jokes and clowned around when he was in comfortable surroundings. He never joined a gang or got in trouble with the law, although he did experiment with alcohol and marijuana.

Brown struggled academically and changed schools several times, but he buckled down and focused on his studies during his senior year. He completed a credit recovery program and graduated from Normandy High School in St. Louis County only eight days before his death. His teachers recalled that he was always the first to arrive for his alternative education classes and expressed an interest in owning a business someday. He signed up to enter a training program for heating and air conditioning repair technicians at Vatterott College.

On August 9, 2014, two days before his vocational classes were scheduled to begin, Brown was shot and killed following an altercation with Darren Wilson, a white officer with the Ferguson Police Department. His body lay in the middle of Canfield Drive for four hours while police investigated the shooting. Peaceful protests and violent riots gripped the city of Ferguson over the next several weeks, as outrage over the shooting of an unarmed black teenager inflamed long-standing racial tensions between the city's primarily black population and its primarily white police force. Wilson's supporters claimed that the shooting was justified because the officer felt threatened by Brown, who matched the description of a suspect in a convenience store robbery that had occurred nearby.

The unrest in Ferguson attracted national media attention. Brown's death served as a catalyst that propelled the growth of the Black Lives Matter (BLM) movement. The hashtag #BlackLivesMatter was used on social media thousands of times, and more than 500 BLM activists from across the country boarded buses for a "freedom ride" to Ferguson in support of the protesters. The Ferguson protests raised awareness of the problem of racial profiling and police brutality toward African Americans and inspired similar actions in other cities.

Although a grand jury declined to indict Wilson, a federal investigation uncovered numerous examples of discriminatory practices by the Ferguson Police Department against black residents.

Brown's funeral was held at Friendly Temple Missionary Baptist Church in St. Louis. Among the 4,500 mourners were the Reverend Jesse Jackson, filmmaker Spike Lee, rapper Sean Combs, and the parents of Trayvon Martin, a black teenager who had been shot to death by a neighborhood watch volunteer in Florida in 2012. President Barack Obama sent personal condolences to Brown's family. Brown's parents eventually retained Benjamin Crump, the attorney who had represented Martin's family, and received a $1.5 million civil wrongful death settlement from the city. In 2016, Lezley McSpadden published a book about her experiences, *Tell the Truth and Shame the Devil: The Life, Legacy, and Love of My Son Michael Brown.*

Sources

John Eligon, "Michael Brown Spent Last Weeks Grappling with Problems and Promise," *New York Times*, August 24, 2014, https://www.nytimes.com/2014/08/25/us/michael-brown-spent-last-weeks-grappling-with-lifes-mysteries.html.

Wesley Lowery and John C. Frankel, "Michael Brown Notched a Hard-Fought Victory Just Days Before He Was Shot: A Diploma," *Washington Post*, August 12, 2014, https://www.washingtonpost.com/politics/mike-brown-notched-a-hard-fought-victory-just-days-before-he-was-shot-a-diploma/2014/08/12/574d65e6-2257-11e4-8593-da634b334390_story.html?utm_term=.7c271d02e84d.

Lezley McSpadden, *Tell the Truth and Shame the Devil: The Life, Legacy, and Love of My Son Michael Brown* (New York: Regan Arts, 2016).

David A. Clarke (1956–)

Former law enforcement official and prominent conservative critic of the Black Lives Matter movement

David Alexander Clarke Jr. was born on August 21, 1956, in Milwaukee, Wisconsin. He was the second of five children born to Jeri Clarke, a school secretary, and David Clarke Sr., who served as a paratrooper with the U.S. Army Rangers during the Korean War and later worked for the U.S. Postal Service. Young David grew up in a structured environment that emphasized respect for authority as well as self-discipline.

He learned personal responsibility from an early age when he was entrusted with packing his father's parachute before recreational skydiving jumps. Clarke enjoyed reading and watching sports as a boy. He kept a scrapbook of newspaper clippings about his uncle, Frank Clarke, who played professional football for the Cleveland Browns and Dallas Cowboys.

Clarke's family lived in mostly white, suburban neighborhood, and he attended a mostly white, Catholic high school. As one of the few African Americans in his social sphere, Clarke endured some racial comments but always made a point of ignoring them. After graduating from high school, Clarke spent one year at the University of Wisconsin at Milwaukee before dropping out to take a job as a truck driver. At the age of 21, he entered the police academy, and in 1978 he joined the Milwaukee Police Department as a patrol officer. Clarke rose steadily through the ranks over the next two decades, serving as a detective and lieutenant in the homicide division before being promoted to captain of a division charged with providing security for local officials and visiting dignitaries. In this role, he became close to Wisconsin's Republican governor, Scott McCallum, who appointed Clarke to the vacant position of Milwaukee County Sheriff in 2002.

Clarke quickly emerged as a prominent political figure. His commanding presence, reputation as a reformer, and authentic, speak-his-mind approach helped him win reelection as sheriff three times. Although Clarke ran as a Democrat in heavily Democratic Milwaukee County, many observers noted that his conservative political and social views aligned more closely with the Republican Party. In response to critics who called him a political opportunist, Clarke insisted that the office of sheriff should be nonpartisan and that his commitment to public safety and law and order transcended politics. Over time, however, Clarke generated controversy by clashing with county officials over budget issues and inviting an evangelical Christian group to proselytize at a mandatory staff meeting. His supervision of the county jail also came under scrutiny when a man died in custody after deputies refused to provide him with drinking water for six days.

During Clarke's 2014 election campaign, the shooting of unarmed black teenager Michael Brown by white police officer Darren Wilson in Ferguson, Missouri, led to nationwide protests against racial bias in law enforcement. The events in Ferguson transformed Black Lives

Matter (BLM) from a hashtag into a social justice movement. Clarke emerged as a vocal critic of BLM on social media and conservative news programs. He denied that police brutality was a serious problem or that law enforcement targeted black citizens. He claimed that black citizens could avoid conflict with police by changing their behavior and being more cooperative. He also argued that protesters' complaints about racial profiling and excessive force bred hostile attitudes toward law enforcement, which made police officers reluctant to do their jobs and put their lives at risk. In 2016 testimony before the House Judiciary Committee, Clarke accused black activists of using racism as an excuse for failures in the black community. He suggested that they should focus their efforts on addressing poverty, crime, and black-on-black violence instead.

During the 2016 presidential election campaign, Clarke expressed strong support for Republican candidate Donald Trump. He was a featured speaker at the Republican National Convention and a frequent guest on conservative talk shows. Clarke continued to create controversy by referring to BLM as a hate group and claiming that protesters would eventually join forces with terrorist organizations like ISIS to take over the United States. Supporters described him as an iconoclast who raised important social issues that no white political figure could mention without being labeled racist. Opponents, on the other hand, portrayed him as a tool used by right-wing extremists to legitimize their bigoted views and validate the conservative backlash against BLM. By the time he resigned as Milwaukee County Sheriff in August 2017, 62 percent of constituents disapproved of his job performance and provocative remarks. Although Clarke's name was frequently mentioned for a job in the Trump administration's Department of Homeland Security, the position fell through when he was accused of plagiarism for failing to cite sources in a master's thesis. As of 2018, Clarke remained a highly paid speaker at conservative fundraising events.

Sources

Jonah Engel Bromwich and Matt Stevens, "Who Is Sheriff Clarke of Milwaukee County?" *New York Times*, May 22, 2017, https://www.nytimes.com/2017/05/22/us/politics/sheriff-david-clarke-bio-facts.html.

Maurice Chammah, "American Sheriff," *Atlantic*, May 5, 2016, https://www.theatlantic.com/politics/archive/2016/05/american-sheriff/481131/.

Kurt Chandler, "The New Black Power," *Milwaukee Magazine*, July 25, 2003, https://www.milwaukeemag.com/the-new-black-power-sheriff-david-clarke/.

Patrisse Cullors (1984–)

Organizer, activist, artist, and cofounder of the Black Lives Matter movement

Patrisse Marie Cullors was born in Los Angeles, California, in 1984. She grew up in the low-income Pacoima neighborhood in the northern San Fernando Valley. Her single mother worked multiple jobs to provide food and shelter for Patrisse and her eight brothers and sisters. At the age of 16, Cullors came out as queer and left home. For the next few years, she sought to understand her place in the world as a young, queer woman of color by reading the works of feminist writers such as Audre Lorde and bell hooks, attending conferences and pride events, exploring her spirituality, and forming connections with other women who were facing similar challenges.

Cullors became a community organizer and political activist in response to her family's experiences with incarceration and police brutality. Her father was in and out of prison on drug charges throughout her youth, while her older brother Monte was beaten and choked by deputies while in custody at the county jail. "My passion is really about looking at the impacts of policing on black communities in particular as well as the impacts incarceration has on black communities," she explained on her website. "I witnessed a lot of state violence, and this movement saved my life." Cullors's organizing work has focused on promoting accountability in law enforcement and building strength and resilience in black communities.

In 2012, Cullors earned a bachelor's degree in religion and philosophy from the University of California at Los Angeles. She also developed a performance art piece called *STAINED: An Intimate Portrayal of State Violence*, which combined stories about her brother's experiences in police custody with information from an American Civil Liberties Union (ACLU) report alleging systematic abuse of inmates at the Los Angeles County Jail. Cullors went on to found Dignity and Justice Now, a nonprofit organization focusing on criminal justice reform. Her efforts paid off when the County of Los Angeles Board of Supervisors approved the creation of a civilian oversight panel for the city's sheriff department and jail system.

In 2013, after neighborhood watch volunteer George Zimmerman was acquitted in the shooting death of unarmed black teenager Trayvon Martin in Florida, Cullors read a Facebook post by her friend and fellow organizer Alicia Garza that concluded with the words "Black Lives Matter." Cullors immediately recognized it as a powerful slogan and turned it into a hashtag, #BlackLivesMatter. She and Garza worked with another activist, Opal Tometi, to create a social media platform around the hashtag, with the goal of using it to galvanize a social justice movement aimed at ending police violence toward African Americans.

In 2014, Black Lives Matter (BLM) moved from social media to the streets of Ferguson, Missouri, to protest the fatal shooting of unarmed black teenager Michael Brown by white police officer Darren Wilson. Following the "freedom ride" that took Cullors and more than 500 activists to Ferguson, BLM grew into an international organization with chapters in dozens of cities. The decentralized, leaderful structure allows individual chapters to focus on social justice campaigns ranging from alleviating poverty and unemployment to improving public education and health care. In 2018, Cullors published a book about her experiences as a BLM cofounder, *When They Call You a Terrorist: A Black Lives Matter Memoir*.

In addition to her work as an organizer, Cullors is a Fulbright scholar and sought-after public speaker. The many awards she has received for her activism include being named a National Association for the Advancement of Colored People (NAACP) History Maker, a *Los Angeles Times* Civil Rights Leader for the Twenty-First Century, and a *Glamour* Woman of the Year. In 2017, according to her website, Cullors was awarded the Sydney Peace Prize "for building a powerful movement for racial equality, courageously reigniting a global conversation around state violence and racism, and harnessing the potential of new platforms and power of people to inspire a bold movement for change at a time when peace is threatened by growing inequality and injustice." Cullors is married to

Janaya Khan, a black transgender activist from Toronto and cofounder of BLM Canada.

Sources

Patrisse Cullors, "Bio," 2018, http://patrissecullors.com/bio/.

Patrisse Cullors, "A Black Lives Matter Leader Opens Up about Marrying Her Partner," *Esquire*, June 24, 2016, http://www.esquire.com/news-politics/a45823/patrisse-cullors-black-gay/.

Abby Sewell, "Activist Battles L.A. County Jailers' Culture of Violence," *Los Angeles Times*, April 14, 2014, http://www.latimes.com/local/la-me-c1-jail-activist-20140414-m-story.html.

Johnetta Elzie (1989–)

Black Lives Matter activist who provided first-person accounts of the Ferguson protests

Johnetta Elzie, known as Netta, was born on April 16, 1989, in North County, St. Louis, Missouri. She grew up in a quiet neighborhood of redbrick ranch homes and enjoyed singing and dancing during family karaoke nights. Throughout her childhood, Elzie spent practically every day hanging out at the beauty shop owned by her mother, Relonda. "It was a safe haven," she recalled in *Complex*, "like a spa for black women. My mom was a therapist, a love doctor, a magician. Women would come in battered and broke, but then they'd get their hair washed, scalp cleaned. My grandma's religious, so some might even get a prayer." Elzie attended Our Lady of Good Counsel, a private school where she was often the only black student, and went on to study journalism at Southeast Missouri State University.

On August 9, 2014, Elzie saw on her Twitter feed that an unarmed black teenager, Michael Brown, had been shot and killed by a white police officer in Ferguson, Missouri, near her childhood home. She arrived on the scene within a few hours and began sharing her observations on social media. Over the next few weeks, Elzie became the most prominent citizen journalist chronicling the massive Ferguson protests from the ground as they happened. She captured photos and videos of the tense situation in the streets, where demonstrators were confronted by heavily armed law enforcement officers with tanks, automatic weapons, Tasers, and tear gas.

As she tracked the unrest in Ferguson, Elzie's base of social media followers expanded to include civil rights heroes, mainstream media outlets, and U.S. Department of Justice (DOJ) officials. Despite her status as an unofficial spokesperson for the emerging Black Lives Matter (BLM) movement, she refused to conform to the respectable image of past generations of civil rights leaders. "I'm not going to stop cursing for the movement or to make people comfortable," she declared in *Essence*. "It actually makes me feel a little better when I can throw in a little colorful language every once in a while. I'm a protester. We resist against the police, so I'm not trying to be cordial and polite with someone who's pointing an M16 in my face."

Elzie worked with fellow activist DeRay Mckesson to produce *This Is the Movement*, a newsletter that provides detailed information, up-to-date statistics, and first-person accounts of incidents of police brutality across the United States. Aimed at social justice advocates, it also features a calendar of protest events and other suggested actions. In 2015, the newsletter received the Howard Zinn Freedom to Write Award from the PEN American Center literary society. Elzie and Mckesson also collaborated with other activists to create We the Protesters, an online tool kit that includes ideas for signs, chants, and lists of demands. To help individuals connect with the movement, they created Stay Woke, an online survey that allows people to input their skills and expertise, identify causes of interest, and volunteer for local efforts to promote equality and social justice.

Along with Mckesson, data analyst Samuel Sinyangwe, and activist Brittany Packnett, Elzie helped compile the Mapping Police Violence database, which features an interactive map of the United States marked with red spots to indicate where an unarmed black person was killed by police. The site also provides personal details for each victim of police violence, including their name, age, photograph, and the story of how they died. In response to critics who claimed that BLM protesters did not offer any positive ideas for change, Elzie joined with other activists to launch Campaign Zero, a website that features a comprehensive slate of policy recommendations aimed at eliminating police violence in the United States. Elzie traced the momentum for all of these initiatives back to the Ferguson protests. "I think that Ferguson has changed things, so that every fatal police shooting that happens has made some type of headline since [then]," she told *Mother Jones*, "in a way where people immediately jump on it, get the facts, or are digging for facts, or are following it and holding people accountable, in a new way that hasn't happened for my generation."

Although Elzie was named one of the world's 50 greatest leaders by *Fortune* magazine, she has also experienced negative aspects to fame. She has often endured threats and harassment on social media, and her movements have been followed by local police since a national cyber and social media security firm labeled her a high-risk "threat actor" in 2015. Elzie lives in Washington, DC, when she is not traveling for speaking engagements or social justice work. When she returns home to St. Louis, she avoids staying with family members because she worries about putting them in danger. "It's frightening to know that you can die for just protesting though it's your first amendment right," she acknowledged in*Jezebel*. "It makes me very numb knowing that that could happen at any moment but you have to come to terms with it. You can't focus on anything else but doing the work and know that if death were to happen, the movement would continue."

Sources

Hillary Crosley Coker, "Activist Johnetta Elzie Talks Ferguson and Black Lives Matter," *Jezebel*, July 17, 2015, https://jezebel.com/activist-johnetta-elzie-talks -ferguson-black-lives-ma-1718374170.

Brandon E. Patterson, "Oppressed People Are Everywhere: A Year after Ferguson, a Conversation with One of the Protests' Organizers," *Mother Jones*, August 7, 2015, http://www.motherjones.com/politics/2015/08/johnetta-elzie-ferguson-black-lives -matter/.

Aaron Randle, "Now You See Me: A Look at the World of Activist Johnetta Elzie," *Complex*, March 8, 2016, http://www.complex.com/life/2016/03/johnetta-elzie -profile.

Bene Viera, "How Activist Johnetta 'Netta' Elzie Speaks Her Truth and What It's Like Fighting for Yours," *Essence*, January 6, 2016, https://www.essence.com /2016/01/06/how-activist-and-essence-cover-star-johnetta-netta-elzie-speaks-her -truth-and-what-its.

Alicia Garza (1981–)

Organizer, activist, writer, and cofounder of the Black Lives Matter movement

Alicia Garza, née Schwartz, was born on January 4, 1981. She grew up in Marin County, California, a wealthy suburb of San Francisco. As the mixed-race daughter of a black woman and a white Jewish man, she always felt different from other people in her mostly white school and community. In that time and place, however, it was understood that "differences shouldn't be talked about because it's uncomfortable," as she recalled in the *Cut*. Garza's first experience with activism came at the age of 12, when her school district debated whether to allow school nurses to dispense condoms to students. Since many of her classmates were already sexually active, Garza supported the idea and was surprised when it ignited a heated controversy over family values.

Garza attended the University of California at San Diego, where she studied anthropology and sociology. She then became a community organizer around such issues as health, fair housing, antiracism, and LGBT rights. In 2009, she became executive director of People Organized to Win Employment Rights (POWER), a San Francisco–based nonprofit organization that helped working-class communities of color combat poverty and racial injustice. During her tenure, POWER fought against gentrification of minority neighborhoods, exposed police brutality against black people, reformed discriminatory policies targeting undocumented immigrants, and secured free public transportation for area youth. Garza was active with other social justice groups as well, including Black Organizing for Leadership and Dignity (BOLD) and Forward Together.

In 2013, when neighborhood watch volunteer George Zimmerman was acquitted in the shooting death of unarmed black teenager Trayvon Martin in Florida, Garza heard the news while sitting in a bar with some friends. "I was in a public place with a lot of other black people," she recalled in the *Nation*. "I felt like I got punched in the gut, but it was like we couldn't look each other in the eye because on televisions across America that court said black lives don't matter." Garza expressed her feelings in a passionate Facebook post that concluded with the words "Black Lives Matter." Her close friend and fellow organizer Patrisse Cullors immediately recognized it as a powerful slo-gan and turned it into a hashtag #BlackLivesMatter. Garza and Cull-ors worked with another activist, Opal Tometi, to create a social media platform around the hashtag, with the goal of using it to galvanize a social justice movement aimed at ending police violence toward Afri-can Americans.

In 2014, Garza took Black Lives Matter (BLM) from social media to the streets of Ferguson, Missouri, to protest the shooting of unarmed black teenager Michael Brown by white police officer Darren Wilson. Using BLM as a rallying cry and organizing tool, she and more than 500 activists from across the country boarded buses for a "freedom ride" to Ferguson in support of the protesters. In Decem-ber 2014, when a grand jury declined to indict Wilson, Garza organ-ized a local BLM protest in which more than a dozen San Francisco activists chained themselves to a Bay Area Rapid Transit train. Their goal was to prevent the train from moving for four hours—the amount of time that Brown's body lay in the street after he was killed—to raise awareness of police violence against black citizens. Although police managed to end the protest after less than two hours, the action received a great deal of media attention.

The Ferguson protests catalyzed the growth of BLM into an international organization. Although Garza was often described as its leader, she oversaw BLM's development as a decentralized, member-led network with dozens of local chapters that were empowered to tar-get the specific issues affecting their communities. From the begin-ning, Garza also emphasized the inclusive nature of the BLM movement, creating an organization that respected and celebrated differences in sexual orientation, gender identity, economic status, immigration status, ability or disability, age, and religion. "We are rejecting a lot of the things that don't work—things that we've done in the past. It's important to not keep doing the same thing over and over, and expect to get different results," she told *Grist*. "Without being disrespectful to the real sacrifices people made, what's real is that this is our generation's time. We're going to do it the way that we know how."

In 2016, Garza became special projects director for the National Domestic Workers Alliance, a nonprofit organization dedicated to securing dignity, fairness, and labor protections for the millions of housekeepers, nannies, and elder care workers in the United States, most of whom are women. She has also written editorials that have appeared in major periodicals and online news sources, including the *Feminist Wire*, the *Guardian*, *Huffington Post*, and the *Nation*. Among the many honors she has received for her activism are a *Glamour* Woman of the Year Award, a *Marie Claire* New Guard Award, a BET Black Girls Rock Award, and the 2017 Sydney Peace Prize. Garza, who identifies as queer, married Malachi Garza, a transgender activist, in 2008. They reside in Oakland, California.

Sources

Ann Friedman, "Don't Try to Do Everything at Once, and Other Advice on Activism from Alicia Garza of Black Lives Matter," *Cut*, September 12, 2017, https://www.thecut.com/2017/09/ann-friedman-interviews-alicia-garza-of-black-lives-matter.html.

Jamilah King, "#BlackLivesMatter: How Three Friends Turned a Spontaneous Facebook Post into a Global Phenomenon," *California Sunday Magazine*, March 1, 2015, https://stories.californiasunday.com/2015-03-01/black-lives-matter/.

Heather Smith, "Meet the BART-Stopping Woman behind Black Lives Matter," *Grist*, December 4, 2014, http://grist.org/politics/stopping-a-bart-train-in-michael-browns-name/.

Mychal Denzel Smith, "A Q&A with Alicia Garza, Co-Founder of #BlackLivesMatter," *Nation*, March 24, 2015, https://www.thenation.com/article/qa-alicia-garza-co-founder-blacklivesmatter/.

DeRay Mckesson (1985–)

Organizer, activist, and spokesperson for the Black Lives Matter movement

DeRay Mckesson was born on July 9, 1985, in Baltimore, Maryland, to drug-addicted parents. After his mother left the family when he was three years old, DeRay and his sister TeRay were raised by their father and great-grandmother in southwestern Baltimore County. Mckesson first became an organizer as a teenager, when he served as chairman of a youth-led nonprofit organization that provided grants to fund community projects. At Catonsville High School, Mckesson was a good student and natural leader who was elected to student council every year. This tradition continued when he attended

Bowdoin, an elite liberal arts college in Maine, and served as president of the student government. Mckesson also worked as a campus tour guide during his college years, and his in-depth knowledge and enthusiastic descriptions of the school's amenities attracted hundreds of new students.

After graduating in 2007 with a degree in government and legal studies, Mckesson joined Teach for America (TFA) and spent two years teaching in low-income public schools in New York City. He then returned to Baltimore to take a job as a special assistant in the office of human capital for the city's public school system. He quickly gained a reputation for putting the welfare of students first in personnel decisions. In 2013, Mckesson moved to Minnesota, where he became a human resources executive in the Minneapolis Public Schools. "Working as a senior leader in two public-school systems changed the way I thought about politics," he noted in *New York Magazine*. "I saw the importance of what it was like to understand the details at such a deep level and how decisions made within the system often have immediate and sweeping impact."

On August 9, 2014, unarmed black teenager Michael Brown was shot and killed by white police officer Darren Wilson in Ferguson, Missouri. Outrage over the controversial shooting, combined with long-standing tension between Ferguson's primarily black population and its primarily white police force, sparked massive protests that garnered national media attention. A week after Brown's death, Mckesson drove nine hours from Minneapolis to Ferguson to support the protesters. He chronicled his experiences, and the process of radicalization he underwent as a result, on social media. "I went to Ferguson initially to bear witness—to compare what I was seeing on TV and Twitter with what was happening in person. I became a protester when I got teargassed for the first time, for simply demanding justice regarding the murder of Mike Brown," he recalled in *New York Magazine*. "It simply wasn't the America that I thought I knew. In those moments, I made a commitment to confront and disrupt until we are able to build equitable systems and structures that support life, and until we are able to end police violence."

Mckesson emerged as one of the most compelling voices documenting the confrontations between protesters and law enforcement in Ferguson. In the spring of 2015, he quit his job to become an organizer in the rapidly growing Black Lives Matter (BLM) movement. In many ways, he became the most visible face of the movement, attending protests across the country in his trademark bright blue Patagonia vest and sharing his observations with a Twitter audience that eventually reached 1 million followers.

Along with fellow activist Johnetta Elzie, whom he met on the streets of Ferguson, Mckesson launched *This Is the Movement*, a newsletter that provides detailed information, up-to-date statistics, and first-person accounts of incidents of police brutality across the United States. Mckesson and Elzie also collaborated to create We the Protesters, an online tool kit that includes ideas for signs, chants, and lists of demands. To help activists connect with the movement, they created Stay Woke, an online survey that allows people to input their skills and expertise, identify causes of interest, and volunteer for local efforts to promote equality and social justice.

Along with Elzie, data analyst Samuel Sinyangwe, and activist Brittany Packnett, Mckesson helped compile the Mapping Police Violence database, which features an interactive map of the United States marked with red spots to indicate where an unarmed black person was killed by police. The site also provides personal details for each victim of police violence, including their name, age, photograph, and the story of how they died. In response to critics who claimed that BLM protesters did not offer any positive ideas for change, Mckesson joined with other activists to launch Campaign Zero, a website that features a slate of policy recommendations aimed at eliminating police violence in America.

As Mckesson became more prominent in the BLM movement, he encountered increased opposition to his presence at protests. Critics accused him of being a paid professional agitator who perpetuated hatred and promoted violence. When Mckesson attended a memorial service for nine black church leaders who were killed by a white supremacist gunman in Charleston, South Carolina, for example, he became the focus of an angry Twitter campaign with the hashtag #GoHomeDeRay. In addition to dealing with online harassment and death threats, Mckesson was also the victim of hackers who took over his e-mail and social media accounts.

In 2016, Mckesson became involved in a high-profile legal battle. It originated when he attended a rally in Baton Rouge, Louisiana, to protest the death of a 37-year-old black man, Alton Sterling, who was shot while he was being restrained on the ground by two white police officers. During the protest, a Baton Rouge police officer was injured by thrown debris. The officer filed a lawsuit against Mckesson and BLM, claiming that they had incited violence against police in retaliation for Sterling's death. After a federal judge dismissed the case in 2017, citing a lack of evidence, Fox News commentator Jeanine Pirro accused Mckesson of "directing the violence" that led to the officer's injury. Mckesson denied the charge, demanded a retraction, and sued for defamation when Fox News refused to comply.

Mckesson ran for mayor of Baltimore in 2016, but he ended up finishing sixth in the Democratic primary. He has received a number of prestigious honors for his activism, including the Peter Jennings Award for Civic Leadership, the Howard Zinn Freedom to Write Award, and the Native Son Award, which honors the achievements of black gay men who defy stereotypes and break down cultural barriers. He also serves as host of a popular podcast, *Pod Save the People*, that discusses politics, culture, and social justice issues.

Sources

Rembert Browne, "In Conversation: DeRay Mckesson," *New York Magazine*, November 22, 2015, http://nymag.com/daily/intelligencer/2015/11/conversation-with-deray-mckesson.html.

Jay Caspian Kang, "Our Demand Is Simple: Stop Killing Us," *New York Times Magazine*, May 4, 2015, https://www.nytimes.com/2015/05/10/magazine/our-demand-is-simple-stop-killing-us.html.

DeRay Mckesson, "Ferguson and Beyond: How a New Civil Rights Movement Began—And Won't End," *Guardian*, August 9, 2015, https://www.theguardian.com/commentisfree/2015/aug/09/ferguson-civil-rights-movement-deray-mckesson-protest.

Brittany Packnett (1985?–)

Educator, activist, and member of President Barack Obama's Task Force on Twenty-First Century Policing

Brittany No'el Packnett was born around 1985 in St. Louis, Missouri. Her father, the Reverend Ronald Packnett, was the pastor at Central Baptist Church, a large, historically black congregation in St. Louis.

Her mother, Gwendolyn Packnett, was a social worker. Brittany and her younger brother, Barrington, were raised in an environment that emphasized the value of education, culture, and political activism. She remembered attending rallies with her parents from the time she was a toddler.

When Brittany was around 10 years old, her father organized a demonstration at the local mall to protest the fact that all of the men hired to portray Santa Claus were white. A local news reporter approached Brittany to ask why she thought it was important to have a black Santa, and she explained that all children should be able to believe that Santa looked like them. "I was raised to know that in the small things and in the large things, the recognition of our community and humanity matters," she explained in *Undefeated*. "Whether or not other people want to acknowledge it or understand it doesn't mean that it's not important."

Packnett spoke out against racism while attending the John Burroughs School, a private, mostly white high school in the affluent St. Louis suburb of Ladue, Missouri. Along with a half-dozen other students of color, she started a diversity organization that gave presentations at school assemblies aimed at increasing racial awareness. Some white students responded negatively to the message, however, including one boy who harassed and spit on her. Packnett went on to earn a bachelor's degree in African American studies from Washington University in St. Louis in 2006, and a master's degree in elementary education from American University in Washington, DC, in 2009. During her college years, she spent a semester serving as a legislative aide for U.S. Representative William Lacy Clay of Missouri.

Packnett built her career as an educator with Teach for America (TFA), a network of leaders dedicated to ending educational inequity. She taught in the District of Columbia public schools for two years and then became executive director of TFA in St. Louis in 2012. Achievements under her leadership included increasing fundraising, launching a local institute, and implementing culturally responsive teaching methods for 20,000 area students. In 2016, she became vice president of national community alliances for the national TFA organization based in Washington, DC.

Packnett's career as an organizer and activist began on August 9, 2014, when an unarmed black teenager named Michael Brown was shot and killed by a white police officer named Darren Wilson in the low-income St. Louis suburb of Ferguson. Outrage over the controversial shooting, combined with long-standing tension between Ferguson's primarily black population and its primarily white police force, sparked massive protests that garnered national media attention. "In a community long overlooked, underserved, and continually harassed by law enforcement, the pressure finally burst the proverbial pipe," Packnett explained in a blog post on the TFA website.

As a longtime resident of the area where Brown was killed, Packnett understood the anger and frustration that permeated Ferguson's black community. Twenty years earlier, her father—despite being a highly respected pastor—had been thrown on the hood of his car and beaten by local police while her five-year-old brother cried in the backseat. Packnett played a key role in planning and coordinating the Ferguson protests, which served as a catalyst for the growth of the Black Lives Matter (BLM) movement. "I didn't set out for this," she noted in *Undefeated*. "I didn't seek fame or visibility. I'm not an entertainer. I'm not an athlete. I'm not someone who said, 'I want to be a star.' I really just love my people a lot. And I love black children a lot. And I want to see us live. I want to see us thrive."

Along with data analyst Samuel Sinyangwe and fellow BLM activists DeRay Mckesson and Johnetta Elzie, Packnett helped compile the Mapping Police Violence database, which features an interactive map of the United States marked with red spots to indicate where an unarmed black person was killed by police. In response to critics who claimed that BLM protesters did not offer any positive ideas for change, Packnett joined with other activists to launch Campaign Zero, a website that features a slate of policy recommendations aimed at eliminating police violence in the United States. In the wake of the Ferguson protests, Missouri Governor Jay Nixon appointed Packnett to serve on the Ferguson Commission, an independent group charged with conducting an in-depth study of the socioeconomic conditions that contributed to Brown's death and the unrest that followed. The commission produced a report, *Forward through Ferguson: A Path toward Racial Equity*, that revealed some of the underlying problems and offered recommendations for improvement.

Packnett was also invited to serve on President Barack Obama's Task Force on Twenty-First Century Policing, an 11-member group that developed policy recommendations intended to improve the relationship between law enforcement and the communities they serve. Obama praised Packnett's contribution to the group in a 2016 commencement address at Howard University: "Some of her fellow activists questioned whether she should participate. [But] she rolled up her sleeves and sat at the same table with big city police chiefs and prosecutors. And because she did, she ended up shaping many of the recommendations of that task force. And those recommendations are now being adopted across the country—changes that many of the protesters called for. If young activists like Brittany had refused to participate out of some sense of ideological purity, then those great ideas would have just remained ideas. But she did participate. And that's how change happens."

Packnett has received a great deal of recognition for her work as an activist, including the Peter Jennings Award for Civic Leadership. She was also named one of *Time* magazine's Twelve New Faces of Black Leadership, one of *Ebony* magazine's Power 100, a member of *Marie Claire*'s New Guard, and number three on Politico's 50 Most Influential list. She serves on the advisory boards of Erase the Hate, an initiative aimed at ridding the world of discrimination, and Rise to Run, an organization dedicated to recruiting progressive women to run for political office. Packnett also contributes a feature called "My Two Cents" to Mckesson's *Pod Save the People* podcast. "Whether it's education or criminal justice reform or police violence or racial injustice, we are dealing fundamentally with people's humanity and making sure that all of our systems and institutions fully recognize it," Packnett said in *Undefeated*. "And that is the business that I'm in, shifting institutions and empowering people to be able to live full lives."

Sources

Kelley D. Evans, "Activist Brittany Packnett Is Woke, and She's Empowering Others Too," *Undefeated*, May 18, 2017, https://theundefeated.com/features/activist-brittany-packnett-is-woke-and-shes-empowering-others-too/.

Brittany Packnett, "Education Didn't Save Michael Brown," Teach for America, August 14, 2014, https://www.teachforamerica.org/top-stories/education-didnt-save-mike-brown-2.

Tiffanie Woods, "Brittany Packnett on the Power of Knowing Your Purpose," *Broadly*, December 25, 2017, https://broadly.vice.com/en_us/article/yw5pkg/brittany-packnett-on-the-power-of-knowing-your-purpose.

Frank Leon Roberts (1983–)

Educator, organizer, political commentator, and creator of the Black Lives Matter syllabus

Frank Leon Roberts was born on August 25, 1983, in Jamaica, Queens, New York. He became a grassroots political organizer during his teen years, when he worked on voter outreach and mobilization efforts following the controversial 2000 presidential election. He cofounded the National Black Justice Coalition in 2004 and was active in a legal campaign to secure racial reparations led by civil rights attorney Johnnie Cochran. Roberts also spent 10 years organizing HIV/AIDS prevention efforts in at-risk black communities in New York City.

After completing a bachelor's degree in 2004 and a master's degree the following year, both at New York University (NYU), Roberts did graduate work at Yale University and became a college professor. He has researched, written, and lectured in the fields of African American literature, art, and performance, race and ethnicity studies, American democracy and politics since the civil rights movement, and modern U.S. social movements. His particular area of academic interest concerns the response to racial injustice in the media, literature, the arts, and everyday life. Roberts has been appointed to teaching positions at the City University of New York, the New School for Social Research, and Princeton University.

In 2015, Roberts introduced a new course entitled Black Lives Matter: Race, Resistance, and Popular Protest at NYU's Gallatin School of Individualized Study. He got the idea for the course by talking with students about race relations in the context of events dominating the news, such as the massive protests against police violence in Ferguson, Missouri, that launched the Black Lives Matter (BLM) movement. "This class was designed as an intervention because there's a tremendous amount of misinformation in terms of the public perception of Black Lives Matter," he said in *Fader*. "In terms of what made it onto the syllabus and how I determined the material, I basically wanted students to be able to leave the class being able to have a dinner table conversation with their parents, or their friends, or whoever."

As one of the first university courses to cover the BLM movement, Roberts's work received national attention. It also proved to be tremendously popular at NYU, where spots filled up quickly and the classroom often overflowed with students auditing the course purely out of interest in the subject matter. Roberts sought to provide his students with tools and context to understand the BLM's history, key players, priorities, demands, and place in the continuum of black struggle in America. "This is not pushing a political agenda, this is saying, 'This story is important to the story of America and the story of American democracy,'" he explained in *Fader*. "And it's also saying that students can't just study Shakespeare and Thoreau or things that happened hundreds of years ago. It's important for them to think critically about the things that are happening today."

In order to inform and educate more people about BLM, Roberts made the syllabus for his course freely available online. He also embarked on a teach-in tour inspired by the Freedom School tradition of the civil rights movement of the 1960s. Since Roberts viewed teaching as a radical form of organizing that had the potential to mobilize progressive communities, his approach was intended to increase the reach of the BLM movement. "I think the legacy of Black Lives Matter is that it will have contributed significantly to the development of American democracy. It's helping America be its best self by pointing to all the places where America currently is *not* its best self," he said in *Fader*. "And the fact that this came from young people, the fact that this movement came from people who were largely not college-educated will have a huge legacy in terms of showing people that everyday people matter. Not just fancy folk, but that everyday people can change a nation and can change the political and cultural climate of a country."

Roberts's groundbreaking work has led to the development of similar courses at institutions of higher learning across the United States, including Dartmouth College, Emory University, the University of Florida, and the University of Michigan. Roberts has shared his perspectives on BLM and racial inequity through numerous media outlets, including BBC Radio, the Chronicle of Higher Education, CNN, *Ebony*, *Huffington Post*, and the *New York Times*. In 2015, he received the Bayard Rustin Award from the Schomburg Center for Research in Black Culture in recognition of his work for racial justice.

Sources

Rawiya Kameir, "Why Frank Leon Roberts's College Course on Black Lives Matter Is So Important," *Fader*, October 11, 2016, http://www.thefader.com/2016/10/11/frank-leon-roberts-nyu-black-lives-matter-syllabus-interview.

Frank Leon Roberts, "Black Lives Matter Syllabus," 2017, http://www.blacklivesmattersyllabus.com/.

Errin Whack, "Ferguson in the Classroom: How One College Took Up Race and Policing This Semester," *Code Switch*, November 8, 2015, https://www.npr.org/sections/codeswitch/2015/11/09/454055691/ferguson-in-the-classroom-how-one-college-took-up-race-and-policing-this-semeste.

Samuel Sinyangwe (1990–)

Data scientist, policy analyst, and creator of the Mapping Police Violence database

Samuel Sinyangwe was born in 1990. His father, Credo Sinyangwe, came to the United States from Tanzania to attend college. His mother, Lisa Early, hailed from a Jewish family that came to the United States to escape the Holocaust in Poland. They met at Cornell University in the late 1970s and eventually got married. Since Sinyangwe's parents often encountered discrimination and harassment as a mixed-race couple, they prepared him for the racism he would experience while growing up in the College Park neighborhood of Orlando, Florida. "I was one of the only black kids in school," he recalled in *Orlando Weekly*, "and I noticed that my sixth-grade teacher always seemed to pick on me for doing things that all the other kids were doing too." Sinyangwe organized his friends to help him document and draw attention to the situation, which contributed to the teacher being fired. "It really embedded within me this sense of agency," he remembered in *Orlando Weekly*, "knowing that if there was a particular injustice, I could do something about it."

Sinyangwe completed the International Baccalaureate program at Winter Park High School in 2008. He went on to study political science at Stanford University in California, with the goal of under-standing the intersection of race with politics, economics, and class. After earning his degree in 2012, Sinyangwe took a position with Pol-icyLink, a San Francisco-based organization dedicated to advancing racial and economic equity. As a program coordinator in the Promise Neighborhoods Institute, he worked to coordinate the efforts of schools, health centers, social services, and families to create supportive communities of opportunity for at-risk children.

Sinyangwe was deeply affected by the 2012 death of Trayvon Martin, an unarmed black teenager who was shot and killed by neigh-borhood watch volunteer George Zimmerman in the Orlando suburb of Sanford, Florida. In his youth, Sinyangwe had attended soccer prac-tice in Sanford and had often stopped at the same convenience store where Martin purchased candy and a fruit drink on the night he was killed. "I was that kid. I could have been Trayvon. That's why it hit me so personally and that's why I realized that needed to be something that took the priority in terms of my focus," he told *Orlando Weekly*. When Zimmerman was acquitted, Sinyangwe decided that "I needed to do something about police violence not only to make myself feel safer, but also to help other people in my generation feel like they weren't just being constantly victimized by these power structures."

Sinyangwe became involved in the Black Lives Matter (BLM) movement in 2014, after another unarmed black teenager, Michael Brown, was shot and killed by a white police officer in Ferguson, Mis-souri. During the massive protests that followed, Sinyangwe sent a message to activist DeRay Mckesson offering to contribute his skills as a data scientist and policy analyst to the cause of ending police vio-lence. In an effort to prove that Brown's death was part of a pattern rather than an isolated incident, Sinyangwe tried to examine federal statistics regarding the number of black citizens killed by police. He learned that the federal government did not have a comprehensive database containing that information. Only about half of the nation's largest police departments reported their numbers to the Federal Bureau of Investigation (FBI) or the U.S. Department of Justice (DOJ), and very few noted the race of the victim, so the government's numbers severely understated the problem.

Sinyangwe set out to compile the data himself. "I looked at two crowd-sourcing databases which collected all of the names. I then went through the media reports listing each of those people who were killed," he explained to BBC News. "I identified whether they were armed or unarmed. I identified them by race by looking at if there was an obituary or another picture of them online." With the help of Mckesson and fellow activists Johnetta Elzie and Brittany Packnett, he created Mapping Police Violence, a website that presented the data in an easy-to-understand visual format. Their work revealed that 30 percent of the 1,152 people killed by police officers in 2015 were black, even though African Americans made up only 13.2 percent of the U.S. population. The data also shed light on large discrepancies in the rate of police-related deaths between different cities and states. Three times as many people were killed by police in Florida than in New York, for instance, even though the states had similar populations.

The Mapping Police Violence database provided BLM activists with a valuable resource to support their arguments and guide their efforts. "We need to be able to hold elected officials and police departments accountable for reducing the numbers of police killings that take place until no more police killings take place," Sinyangwe told MTV News. "And the only way we can do that is with the data, by tracking trends over time."

In response to critics who claimed that BLM protesters did not suggest any positive ideas for addressing the problem of police violence, Sinyangwe and other activists created Campaign Zero, a comprehensive platform of policy solutions aimed at reducing the number of people killed by police nationwide to zero. It included 10 major areas of suggested reform measures, such as establishing civilian review boards to oversee police departments, requiring officers to wear body cameras, eliminating fees and fines for minor infractions, and prohibiting the purchase of military surplus equipment by police departments.

In 2016, Sinyangwe emerged as a vocal critic of the Ferguson effect, a theory claiming that police had become less aggressive in performing their jobs since widespread BLM protests had raised concerns about the use of force. Some law enforcement officials claimed that the intense public scrutiny led to lax policing, which emboldened criminals and caused a surge in violent crime. To debunk this theory, Sinyangwe pointed to data showing that the rate of police-involved deaths had increased since 2014. "Even if we assume that police are behaving less aggressively (except when they decide to use deadly force), it's not clear why this would lead to increased crime unless you assume that aggressive police officers are the solution to keeping our communities safe," he wrote in the *Guardian*. "If police can't do their jobs without violating the constitutional rights of black people, then we must question the institution of policing rather than the protesters who expose its transgressions."

Sources

Monivette Cordeiro, "How an Orlando Data Scientist Is Helping #BlackLivesMatter Make the Case against Police Violence," *Orlando Weekly*, March 23, 2016, https://www.orlandoweekly.com/orlando/how-an-orlando-data-scientist-is-helping-the-blacklivesmatter-movement-make-the-case-against-police-violence/Content?oid=2478826.

Kristina Marusic, "This Map of Police Violence Aims to Create a Path to Justice," MTV News, April 15, 2015, http://www.mtv.com/news/2133351/map-police-violence/.

Samuel Sinyangwe, "Giving the Ferguson Effect a New Name Won't Make It Truer," *Guardian*, May 13, 2016, https://www.theguardian.com/commentisfree/2016/may/13/ferguson-effect-james-comey-fbi-policing.

Opal Tometi (1984–)

Organizer, communication strategist, and cofounder of the Black Lives Matter movement

Opal Tometi was born in 1984 in Phoenix, Arizona. She was the oldest of three children born to Nigerian parents who came to the United States seeking a better future for themselves. Tometi grew up within a large, close-knit Nigerian community, where many people wore traditional, brightly colored clothing and celebrated their African heritage and culture. In this environment, however, she also witnessed the impact of anti-immigrant sentiment and policies. When she was in high school, for instance, her best friend's mother was sent to an immigration detention center and then deported. Since the mother was a widow, her four young daughters—who were U.S. citizens—were left to the care of other Nigerian families in Phoenix. "I learned a lot about my own community and our ability to take care of one another, even when the government tears our families apart," Tometi recalled in *Coveteur.*

After graduating from high school, where she performed as a member of the step team, Tometi attended the University of Arizona, earning a bachelor's degree in history in 2005. After college, she worked as a case manager for survivors of domestic violence. In 2010, she received a master's degree in communications and advocacy from Arizona State University. That same year, Arizona enacted one of the toughest anti-immigration laws in the country. SB 1070 required non-U.S. citizens to register upon entering the state and carry immigration papers with them at all times. It also included the controversial "show me your papers" provision, which required state police to ascertain the immigration status of anyone they stopped for any reason. When organizers with the Black Alliance for Just Immigration (BAJI) came to Phoenix to help black and Latino immigrants who were affected by the law, Tometi joined the group as a national organizer. In 2013, she moved to New York City to become executive director of BAJI. In this role, she attended a congressional briefing on black immigrants and organized a rally for immigrant justice.

Tometi's involvement with Black Lives Matter (BLM) began in 2013, when a jury acquitted neighborhood watch volunteer George Zimmerman in the fatal shooting of unarmed black teenager Trayvon Martin in Florida. Thinking of her younger brothers, Tometi was deeply affected by the outcome of the highly publicized trial. "When I heard that verdict I cried like I had never cried before," she recalled in the *Daily Item.* "It struck me that for black people, this would be our story of the century. Trayvon Martin was put on trial for his own murder, and when Zimmerman was found not guilty I was inconsolable." Rather than dwell on her feelings of anger and hopelessness, however, she immediately started looking for ways to organize a response and bring meaning to Martin's death.

Tometi found the opportunity she was looking for on her Twitter feed, where fellow organizers Alicia Garza and Patrisse Cullors had begun using the hashtag #BlackLivesMatter. She was struck by the simplicity and power of the words, which seemed to articulate a vision for the future. She worked with Garza and Cullors to develop a social media platform and communication strategy around the hashtag, with the hopes of using it to galvanize a social justice movement. "[Black

Lives Matter] was created out of a profound sense of black love," Tometi explained in the *California Sunday Magazine*. "We wanted to affirm to our people that we love one another, and that no matter how many times we hear about the extrajudicial killing of a community member, we would mourn, and affirm the value of their life."

Tometi and her fellow activists took the hashtag from social media to the streets of Ferguson, Missouri, in 2014 to protest the fatal shooting of another unarmed black teenager, Michael Brown, by a white police officer. The Ferguson protests sparked demonstrations across the country and catalyzed the growth of the BLM movement. As a cofounder of the movement, Tometi has emphasized that African American liberation requires wide-reaching, systemic change. "I think what we're seeing right now is a crisis of our democracy, and the reality is that these types of actions that we're seeing—the disruptions, the really courageous acts of nonviolent civil disobedience that are just taking this country by storm, really—is an effort to call attention to a very real crisis that's happening in our communities," Tometi told the *Atlantic*. "Our communities are reeling from poverty, from unemployment, from discrimination of all sorts and different interactions that they're having with the law enforcement, and education system, and so on."

In recognition of her work as an organizer and activist, Tometi has received a number of awards and honors. She was included on *Cosmopolitan*'s list of the Top 100 Extraordinary Women, on the Root 100 list of African American achievers between the ages of 25 and 45, and among the world's 50 greatest leaders by *Politico* and *Fortune*. Along with her BLM cofounders, she received BET's Black Girls Rock Community Change Agent Award and a Webby Award for Social Movement of the Year. Tometi resides in Brooklyn, New York, where she enjoys riding her single-speed bicycle and collecting African art.

Sources

Rick Dandes, "How Three Friends Tapped the Power of Social Media to Start a Movement," *Daily Item*, September 21, 2015, http://www.dailyitem.com/news/ how-friends-tapped-power-of-social-media-to-start-a/article_377ddf64-60d3-11e5 -93f3-b3d056ce6798.html.

Jamilah King, "#BlackLivesMatter: How Three Friends Turned a Spontaneous Facebook Post into a Global Phenomenon," *California Sunday Magazine*, March 1, 2015, https://stories.californiasunday.com/2015-03-01/black-lives-matter/.

Emily Ramshaw, "A Black Lives Matter Co-Founder on How Immigration Policy in Trump's America Is Different—And the Same," *Coveteur*, February 22, 2017, http://coveteur.com/2017/02/22/black-lives-matter-co-founder-opal-tometi -immigration-justice/.

Scott Stossel, "Washington Ideas Forum 2015: How #BlackLivesMatter Went Viral," *Atlantic*, October 15, 2015, https://www.theatlantic.com/video/index/ 410644/how-blacklivesmatter-went-viral/.

Primary Documents

New York Mayor Bill de Blasio Reflects on Eric Garner's Death

In December 2014, a Staten Island grand jury declined to indict the New York Police Department officers involved in the chokehold death of Eric Garner. In an emotional speech, New York Mayor Bill de Blasio expresses determination to resolve the crisis of police violence and ensure the safety of black men—like his biracial son, Dante—in encounters with law enforcement.

It's a very emotional day for our city. It's a very painful day for so many New Yorkers. That is the core reality. So many people in this city are feeling pain right now. And we're grieving, again, over the loss of Eric Garner, who was a father, a husband, a son, a good man—a man who should be with us, and isn't. That pain, that simple fact, is felt again so sharply today.

I spent some time with Ben Garner, Eric's father, who is in unspeakable pain. And it's a very hard thing to spend time trying to comfort someone you know is beyond the reach of comfort because of what he's been through. I can only imagine. I couldn't help but immediately think what it would mean to me to lose [my son] Dante.

Life could never be the same thereafter, and I could feel how it will never be whole again—things will never be whole again for Mr. Garner. And even in the midst of his pain, one of the things he stopped and said so squarely was, there can't be violence. He said Eric would not have wanted violence, violence won't get us anywhere. He was so sharp and clear in his desire, despite his pain. I found it noble. I could only imagine what it took for him to summon that. No family should have to go through what the Garner family went through.

And the tragedy is personal to this family, but it's become something personal to so many of us. It's put in stark perspective the relationship between police and community. This issue has come to the fore again, and we have to address them with all our might. We can't stop. We have to act, with the assumption that it's all of our jobs to never have a tragedy again—that's what we have to fight for.

This is profoundly personal for me. I was at the White House the other day, and the President of the United States turned to me, and he met Dante a few months ago, and he said that Dante reminded him of what he looked like as a teenager. And he said, I know you see this crisis through a very personal lens. I said to him I did. Because [my wife] Chirlane [McCray] and I have had to talk to Dante for years, about the dangers he may face. A good young man, a law-abiding young man, who would never think to do anything wrong, and yet, because of a history that still hangs over us, the dangers he may face—we've had to literally train him, as families have all over this city for decades, in how to take special care in any encounter he has with the police officers who are there to protect him.

And that painful sense of contradiction that our young people see first—that our police are here to protect us, and we honor that, and at the same time, there's a history we have to overcome, because for so many of our young people, there's a fear. And for so many of our families, there's a fear. So I've had to worry, over the years, Chirlane's had to worry—was Dante safe each night? There are so many families in this city who feel that each and every night—is my child safe? And not just from some of the painful realities—crime and violence in some of our neighborhoods—but are they safe from the very people they want to have faith in as their protectors? That's the reality. And it conforms to something bigger that you've heard come out in the protests in Ferguson, and all over the country.

This is now a national moment of grief, a national moment of pain, and searching for a solution, and you've heard in so many places, people of all backgrounds, utter the same basic phrase. They've said "Black Lives Matter." And they said it because it had to be said. It's a phrase that should never have to be said—it should be self-evident. But our history, sadly, requires us to say that Black Lives Matter. Because, as I said the other day, we're not just dealing with a problem in 2014, we're not dealing with years of racism leading up to it, or decades of racism—we are dealing with centuries of racism that have brought us to this day. That is how profound the crisis is. And that is how fundamental the task at hand is, to turn from that history and to make a change that is profound and lasting. . . .

Here in this city, change is happening. Even in this moment, people are feeling pain and frustration and confusion. Change is happening right now and I said in the meeting change is happening because the people willed it to happen. We're leaders, we all strive to serve and help our people, but the people willed this change to happen. The people believed the broken policy of stop and frisk had to end and it has ended. The people believed there were too many young people of color arrested and saddled with a record for the rest of their lives simply for the possession of a small amount of marijuana and that policy has been changed. The people demanded something different. It's my responsibility and responsibility to everyone standing here with me to achieve that on behalf of the people. . . .

I have to emphasize, and we've seen this all over the country, but I know it's true here, and I have an experience from last year that I think is evidence. This is not just a demand coming from the African American community. It's not just a demand coming from the Latino community. It's coming from every community. It's coming from people from all faiths who want a city of fairness, who want violence to end, who want no family to go through the tragedy the Garners did.

So, people will express themselves now, as they should in a democracy. I ask everyone to listen to what Ben Garner said and what Eric Garner's son said as well—if you really want a dignified life of Eric Garner, you will do so through peaceful protest. You will work relentlessly for change. You will not sully his name with violence or vandalism. That doesn't bring us closer to a better community. The only thing that has ever worked is peaceful protest. Non-violent social activism is the only thing that has ever worked.

And the Garner family has made the abundantly clear. Michael Brown's family made that abundantly clear. People should listen to those we say we stand in solidarity with, fulfill their wishes and work for change the right way. . . .

Source: "Transcript: Mayor de Blasio Holds Media Availability at Mt. Sinai United Christian Church on Staten Island," NYC, December 3, 2014, http://www1.nyc.gov /office-of-the-mayor/news/542-14/transcript-mayor-de-blasio-holds-media -availability-mt-sinai-united-christian-church-staten.

Attorney General Eric Holder Releases "Searing" Ferguson Report

Following the fatal shooting of unarmed black teenager Michael Brown by Officer Darren Wilson in Ferguson, Missouri, the U.S. Department of Justice launched an investigation of the Ferguson Police Department. Attorney General Eric Holder announced the results on March 4, 2015. While federal investigators did not find enough evidence to charge Wilson with a crime, they uncovered a pattern of law enforcement practices that violated black residents' civil rights, created an atmosphere of fear and mistrust, and helped explain "how a single tragic incident set off the city of Ferguson like a powder keg."

I recognize that the findings in our report may leave some to wonder how the department's findings can differ so sharply from some of the initial, widely reported accounts of what transpired. I want to emphasize that the strength and integrity of America's justice system has always rested on its ability to deliver impartial results in precisely these types of difficult circumstances—adhering strictly to the facts and the law, regardless of assumptions. Yet it remains not only valid—but essential—to question how such a strong alternative version of events was able to take hold so swiftly, and be accepted so readily.

A possible explanation for this discrepancy was uncovered during the course of our *second* federal investigation, conducted by the Civil Rights Division to determine whether Ferguson Police officials have engaged in a widespread pattern or practice of violations of the U.S. Constitution or federal law.

As detailed in our searing report—also released by the Justice Department today—this investigation found a community that was deeply polarized; a community where deep distrust and hostility often characterized interactions between police and area residents.

A community where local authorities consistently approached law enforcement *not* as a means for protecting public safety, but as a way to generate revenue. A community where both policing and municipal court practices were found to disproportionately harm African American residents. A community where this harm frequently appears to stem, at least in part, from racial bias—both implicit and explicit. And a community where all of these conditions, unlawful practices, and constitutional violations have not only severely undermined the public trust, eroded police legitimacy, and made local residents less safe—but created an intensely charged atmosphere where people feel under assault and under siege *by those charged to serve and protect them.*

Of course, violence is never justified. But seen in this context— amid a highly toxic environment, defined by mistrust and resentment, stoked by years of bad feelings, and spurred by illegal and misguided practices—it is not difficult to imagine how a single tragic incident set off the city of Ferguson like a powder keg. In a sense, members of the community may not have been responding only to a single isolated confrontation, but also to a pervasive, corrosive, and deeply unfortunate lack of trust—attributable to numerous constitutional violations by their law enforcement officials including First Amendment abuses, unreasonable searches and seizures, and excessive and dangerous use of force; exacerbated by *severely disproportionate* use of these tactics against African Americans; and driven by overriding pressure from the city to use law enforcement not as a public service, but as a tool for raising revenue.

According to our investigation, this emphasis on revenue generation through policing has fostered unconstitutional practices—or practices that contribute to constitutional violations—at nearly every level of Ferguson's law enforcement system. Ferguson police officers issued nearly 50 percent more citations in the last year than they did in 2010—an increase that has *not* been driven, or even accompanied, by a rise in crime.

As a result of this excessive reliance on ticketing, today, the city generates a significant amount of revenue from the enforcement of code provisions. Along with taxes and other revenue streams, in 2010, the city collected over $1.3 million in fines and fees collected by the court. For fiscal year 2015, Ferguson's city budget anticipates fine revenues to exceed $3 million—more than double the total from just five years prior. Our review of the evidence, and our conversations with police officers, have shown that significant pressure is brought to bear on law enforcement personnel to deliver on these revenue increases. Once the system is primed for maximizing revenue—starting with fines and fine enforcement—the city relies on the police force to serve, essentially, as a collection agency for the municipal court rather than a law enforcement entity focused primarily on maintaining and promoting public safety. And a wide variety of tactics, including disciplinary measures, are used to ensure certain levels of ticketing by individual officers, regardless of public safety needs.

As a result, it has become commonplace in Ferguson for officers to charge multiple violations for the same conduct. Three or four charges for a single stop is considered fairly routine. Some officers even compete to see who can issue the largest number of citations during a single stop—a total that, in at least one instance, rose as high as *14*. And we've observed that even minor code violations can sometimes result in multiple arrests, jail time and payments that exceed the cost of the original ticket many times over. . . .

Over time, it's clear that this culture of enforcement actions being disconnected from the public safety needs of the community—and often to the detriment of community residents—has given rise to a disturbing and unconstitutional pattern or practice. Our investigation showed that Ferguson police officers routinely violate the Fourth Amendment in stopping people without reasonable suspicion, arresting them without probable cause, and using unreasonable force against them. According to the Police Department's *own records*, its officers frequently infringe on residents' First Amendment rights. They interfere with the right to record police activities. And they make enforcement decisions based on the way individuals express themselves.

Many of these constitutional violations have become routine. For instance, even though it's illegal for police officers to detain a person—even briefly—without reasonable suspicion, it's become common practice for officers in Ferguson to stop pedestrians and request identification for no reason at all. And even in cases where police encounters start off as constitutionally defensible, we found that they frequently and rapidly escalate—and end up blatantly and unnecessarily crossing the line. . . .

Our investigation showed that members of Ferguson's police force frequently escalate, rather than defuse, tensions with the residents they encounter. And such actions are sometimes accompanied by First Amendment violations—including arresting people for talking back to officers, recording their public activities, or engaging in other conduct that is constitutionally protected.

This behavior not only exacerbates tensions in its own right; it has the effect of stifling community confidence that's absolutely vital for effective policing. And this, in turn, deepens the widespread distrust provoked by the department's other unconstitutional exercises of police power—none of which is more harmful than its pattern of excessive force.

Among the incidents of excessive force discovered by our comprehensive review, some resulted from stops or arrests that had no legal basis to begin with. Others were punitive or retaliatory in nature. The police department's routine use of Tasers was found to be not merely unconstitutional, but abusive and dangerous. Records showed a disturbing history of using unnecessary force against people with mental illness. And our findings indicated that the overwhelming majority of force—almost *90 percent*—is directed against African Americans.

This deeply alarming statistic points to one of the most pernicious aspects of the conduct our investigation uncovered: that these policing practices disproportionately harm African American residents. In fact, our review of the evidence found *no* alternative explanation for the disproportionate impact on African American residents other than implicit and explicit racial bias. . . .

The evidence of racial bias comes not only from statistics, but also from remarks made by police, city and court officials. A thorough examination of the records—including a large volume of work emails—shows a number of public servants expressing racist comments or gender discrimination; demonstrating grotesque views and images of African Americans in which they were seen as the "other," called "transient" by public officials, and characterized as lacking personal responsibility.

I want to emphasize that *all* of these examples, statistics and conclusions are drawn directly from the exhaustive Findings Report that the Department of Justice has released. Clearly, these findings—and others included in the report—demonstrate that, although some community perceptions of Michael Brown's tragic death may not have been accurate, the widespread conditions that these perceptions were based upon, and the climate that gave rise to them, were all too real.

This is a reality that our investigators repeatedly encountered in their interviews of police and city officials, their conversations with local residents, and their review of thousands of pages of records and documents. This evidence pointed to an unfortunate and unsustainable situation that has not only severely damaged relationships between law enforcement and members of the community, but made professional policing vastly more difficult—and unnecessarily placed officers at increased risk. And today—now that our investigation has reached its conclusion—it is time for Ferguson's leaders to take immediate, wholesale and structural corrective action. Let me be clear: the United States Department of Justice reserves all its rights and abilities to force compliance and implement basic change.

The report from the Justice Department presents two sets of immediate recommendations—for the Ferguson Police Department and the Municipal Court. These recommendations include the implementation of a robust system of true community policing; increased tracking, review and analysis of Ferguson Police Department stop, search, ticketing and arrest practices; increased civilian involvement in police decision-making; and the development of mechanisms to effectively respond to allegations of officer misconduct. They also involve changes to the municipal court system including modifications to bond amounts and detention procedures; an end to the use of arrest warrants as a means of collecting owed fines and fees; and compliance with due process requirements. Ensuring meaningful, sustainable and verifiable reform will require that these and other measures be part of a court-enforceable remedial process that includes involvement from community stakeholders as well as independent oversight in order to remedy the conduct we have identified, to address the underlying culture we have uncovered, and to restore and rebuild the trust that has been so badly eroded.

As the brother of a retired police officer, I know that the overwhelming majority of America's brave men and women in law enforcement do their jobs honorably, with integrity, and often at great personal risk. I have immense regard for the vital role that they play in all of America's communities—and the sacrifices that they and their families are too often called to make on behalf of their country. It is in great part for their sake—and for their safety—that we must seek to rebuild trust and foster mutual understanding in Ferguson and in all communities where suspicion has been allowed to fester. Negative practices by individual law enforcement officers and individual departments present a significant danger not only to their communities, but also to committed and hard-working public safety officials around the country who perform incredibly challenging jobs with unwavering professionalism and uncommon valor. Clearly, we owe it to these brave men and women to ensure that all law enforcement officials have the tools, training and support they need to do their jobs with maximum safety and effectiveness. . . .

I have repeatedly seen that—although the concerns we are focused on today may be particularly acute in Ferguson—they are not confined to any one city, state, or geographic region. They implicate questions about fairness and trust that are national in scope. And they point *not* to insurmountable divides between people of different perspectives, but to the shared values—and the common desire for peace, for security, and for public safety—that binds together police *as well as* protestors. . . .

Source: Eric H. Holder Jr., "Attorney General Holder Delivers Update on Investigations in Ferguson, Missouri," March 4, 2015, U.S. Department of Justice, Civil Rights Division, https://www.justice.gov/opa/speech/attorney-general-holder -delivers-update-investigations-ferguson-missouri.

Sheriff David A. Clarke Defends Law Enforcement

In the wake of massive protests over the deaths of unarmed black men at the hands of police, the House Judiciary Committee held a hearing on law enforcement reform in May 2015. One of the people invited to speak at the hearing was Milwaukee County Sheriff David A. Clarke, who had gained national prominence as a critic of the Black Lives Matter movement. The following excerpt includes Clarke's prepared testimony as well as his questioning by Representative Hakeem Jeffries of New York.

Sheriff CLARKE. Since the events that led to riots in Ferguson, Missouri, police use of force has become scrutinized nationally. Police use of force should be scrutinized—locally, that is. It should be examined in terms of factual data and circumstances that led to the police action and not from the emotional foundation of false narratives or catchy slogans like, "hands up, don't shoot," "no justice, no peace," or "Black lives matter." Let us leave that conduct for the public to engage in, not the mainstream media or those elected officials who cannot resist the opportunity to exploit the emotions of an uninformed or misinformed public simply for political gain. . . .

Black-on-Black crime is the elephant in the room that few want to talk about. We could talk about the police use of force, but it does not start with transforming the police profession. It starts by asking why we need so much assertive policing in the American ghetto. Are police officers perfect? Not by any stretch of the imagination. Are police agencies perfect? Not even close. But we are the best that our communities have to offer.

Instead, the conversation should be about transforming Black underclass subculture behavior. The discussion must start with addressing the behavior of people who have no respect for authority, who fight with and try to disarm the police, who flee the police, and who engage in other flawed lifestyle choices.

Bashing the police is the low-hanging fruit. It is easier to talk about the rare killing—fortunately, rare—of a Black male by police because emotion can be exploited for political advantage. The police are easier to throw overboard because they cannot fight back politically. This, however, is counterproductive and will lead to police pulling back in high-crime areas where good, law-abiding Black people live. Black people will be the losers in all this as violent crime rates skyrocket over time. This means more Black crime victims.

Economist and author Thomas Sowell, a man I admire, said this about policing: "If people who are told that they under arrest, and who refuse to come with the police, cannot be forcibly taken into custody, then we do not have the rule of law when the law itself is downgraded to suggestions that no one has the power to enforce."

Sowell further pointed out that, "for people who have never tried to take into custody somebody resisting arrest, to sit back in the safety and comfort of their homes or offices and second guess people who face the dangers inherent in that process—dangers for both the officer and the person under arrest—is yet another example of the irresponsible self-indulgences of our time." . . .

Mr. JEFFRIES. Thank you, Mr. Chairman. Thank you for your work on criminal justice reform, as well, as we try to work toward a productive resolution of the challenges we face here in America. I think most would agree that, in a democracy, we just need a balance between effective law enforcement on the one hand and a healthy respect for the Constitution, for civil rights, and for civil liberties on the other. What people want in inner city communities like those I represent, or as Sheriff Clarke would refer to as the ghetto, what people want is to make sure that the constitutional principle of equal protection under the law applies to everyone. There is concern that, in certain instances, that is not the case. The overwhelmingly majority of police officers are hardworking individuals who are there to protect and serve the community. That is my position. I believe that is the position of everyone who is genuinely interested in police reform. But we cannot ignore the fact that we have a problem in some instances with excessive use of police force, and the fact that often it is the case that when a police officer crosses the line, they are not held accountable by the criminal justice system. That creates consequences in terms of a distrust in many communities, perhaps leading to the absence of cooperation. Let me start with Sheriff Clarke. You mentioned in your testimony that Black-on-Black crime is the elephant in the room that few want to talk about. Is that correct?

Sheriff CLARKE. Yes, sir.

Mr. JEFFRIES. We have had a very robust discussion about it today. Have you been satisfied? It has come up several times.

Sheriff CLARKE. Not at all.

Mr. JEFFRIES. Okay, you are not satisfied. Now, I agree it is a problem. Eighty percent of Whites kill Whites, correct?

Sheriff CLARKE. I won't dispute that figure.

Mr. JEFFRIES. Okay. Actually, it is 83 percent. Now, is White-on-White violence a problem in America that we should also have a robust discussion about?

Sheriff CLARKE. Mr. Chair, Congressman, violence in America, in general, is problematic. But if you look at the rates, that is where it starts coming a little more into balance in terms of the data I have seen, and I have looked at a lot of it. The White-on-White crime does happen at the 80 percent figure you put out there, but when you look at the rates of it, these two are not even close.

Mr. JEFFRIES. The rates are roughly equivalent in terms of the context of people who live next to each other, and because of housing, segregation patterns, or just where people tend to live in America, ethnic violence, racial violence, tends to occur within the same group. So elevating it beyond that fact I think is irresponsible. We all want to deal with the Black-on-Black violence problem. It was mentioned that there is a cooperation issue in the Black-on-Black violence context. I do not think I have heard the phrase "blue wall of silence" mentioned here. So if we are going to have a conversation about cooperation, when someone crosses the line, it seems to me to make sense that we also have to deal with what may be another elephant in the room, to use your term, Sheriff Clarke, the blue wall of silence. The overwhelmingly majority of officers are good officers, but what often occurs is that when an officer crosses the line, the ethic is not to cooperate or participate or speak on what a bad apple officer has done. ... Sheriff Clarke, you also mentioned the use of force should be examined in terms of factual data and not an emotional foundation of false narratives. Is that correct? Did I get your testimony correct in that regard?

Sheriff CLARKE. Mr. Chair, Congressman, yes.

Mr. JEFFRIES. Okay. Now, was the reaction to the Eric Garner case, who was choked to death using a procedure that had been banned by the NYPD for more than twenty years, wasn't resisting arrest, said, "I can't breathe" eleven times, eleven different occasions, there was no response by all of the police officers there, was that a false narrative that people in the City of New York and the country are reacting to, sir?

Sheriff CLARKE. Mr. Chair, Congressman, first of all, he was not choked to death, not from the report I had seen out of the grand jury testimony and even from the medical examiner's report. He wasn't choked to death.

Mr. JEFFRIES. The medical examiner ruled the death a homicide by asphyxiation. In the ghetto, that is called being called choked to death, sir.

Sheriff CLARKE. Well, we can have this discussion later on about the facts, because we could be here for a while. My understanding is he died of a heart attack, okay? But anyway, you said he was not resisting arrest. He was resisting arrest. He was told that he was under arrest and put his hands behind his back, and he would not do so. That is why I put in my remarks here, the reference from Thomas Sowell about when law enforcement officers tell someone they are under arrest and they cannot use force to execute that arrest, we do not have the rule of law when it is merely a suggestion for them that they are going to jail or to put their hands behind their back. Those are behaviors, like in the instance of Mike Brown in Ferguson, Missouri, where some different choices by the individual could have helped the situation. In other words, Mike Brown was just simply told to get out of the street.

Mr. JEFFRIES. Sir, my time has expired. But for you to come here and testify essentially that Eric Garner is responsible for his own death when he was targeted by police officers for allegedly selling loose cigarettes, which is an administrative violation for which he got the death penalty, is outrageous. If we are going to have a responsible conversation, we have to at least agree on a common set of reasonable facts that all Americans interpret, particularly in this instance, because they caught the whole thing on videotape.

Source: "Policing Strategies for the Twenty-First Century," Hearing before the Committee on the Judiciary, House of Representatives, 114th Congress, May 19, 2015, pp. 5–7, 101–103, https://judiciary.house.gov/wp-content/uploads/2016/02/114-29_94653.pdf.

Federal Investigators Find Police Bias in Baltimore

The death of Freddie Gray in April 2015 from spinal injuries sustained while in police custody sparked a series of protests in the city of Baltimore. Eighteen months later, the results of a U.S. Department of Justice investigation showed a pattern of racially biased practices by the Baltimore City Police Department.

Today, we announce the outcome of the Department of Justice's investigation of the Baltimore City Police Department (BPD).

After engaging in a thorough investigation, initiated at the request of the City of Baltimore and BPD, the Department of Justice concludes that there is reasonable cause to believe that BPD engages in a pattern or practice of conduct that violates the Constitution or federal law. BPD engages in a pattern or practice of:

(1) making unconstitutional stops, searches, and arrests;
(2) using enforcement strategies that produce severe and unjustified disparities in the rates of stops, searches and arrests of African Americans;

(3) using excessive force; and

(4) retaliating against people engaging in constitutionally-protected expression.

This pattern or practice is driven by systemic deficiencies in BPD's policies, training, supervision, and accountability structures that fail to equip officers with the tools they need to police effectively and within the bounds of the federal law.

We recognize the challenges faced by police officers in Baltimore and other communities around the country. Every day, police officers risk their lives to uphold the law and keep our communities safe. Investigatory stops, arrests, and force—including, at times, deadly force—are all necessary tools used by BPD officers to do their jobs and protect the safety of themselves and others. Providing policing services in many parts of Baltimore is particularly challenging, where officers regularly confront complex social problems rooted in poverty, racial segregation and deficient educational, employment and housing opportunities. Still, most BPD officers work hard to provide vital services to the community.

The pattern or practice occurs as a result of systemic deficiencies at BPD. The agency fails to provide officers with sufficient policy guidance and training; fails to collect and analyze data regarding officers' activities; and fails to hold officers accountable for misconduct. BPD also fails to equip officers with the necessary equipment and resources they need to police safely, constitutionally, and effectively. Each of these systemic deficiencies contributes to the constitutional and statutory violations we observed. . . .

In the course of our investigation, we learned there is widespread agreement that BPD needs reform. Almost everyone who spoke to us—from current and former City leaders, BPD officers and command staff during ride-alongs and interviews, community members throughout the many neighborhoods of Baltimore, union representatives of all levels of officers in BPD, advocacy groups, and civic and religious leaders—agrees that BPD has significant problems that have undermined its efforts to police constitutionally and effectively. As we note in this report, many of these people and groups have documented those problems in the past, and although they may disagree about the nature, scope, and solutions to the challenges, many have also made efforts to address them.

Nevertheless, work remains, in part because of the profound lack of trust among these groups, and in particular, between BPD and certain communities in Baltimore. The road to meaningful and lasting reform is a long one, but it can be taken. This investigation is intended to help Baltimore take a large step down this path.

Recent events highlight the critical importance of mutual trust and cooperation between law enforcement officers and the people they serve. A commitment to constitutional policing builds trust that enhances crime fighting efforts and officer safety. Conversely, frayed community relationships inhibit effective policing by denying officers important sources of information and placing them more frequently in dangerous, adversarial encounters. We found these principles in stark relief in Baltimore, where law enforcement officers confront a long history of social and economic challenges that impact much of the City, including the perception that there are "two Baltimores:" one wealthy and largely white, the second impoverished and predominantly black.

Community members living in the City's wealthier and largely white neighborhoods told us that officers tend to be respectful and responsive to their needs, while many individuals living in the City's largely African-American communities informed us that officers tend to be disrespectful and do not respond promptly to their calls for service. Members of these largely African-American communities often felt they were subjected to unjustified stops, searches, and arrests, as well as excessive force. These challenges amplify the importance of using policing methods that build community partnerships and ensure fair and effective enforcement without regard for affluence or race through robust training, close supervision, data collection and analysis, and accountability for misconduct.

Starting in at least the late 1990s, however, City and BPD leadership responded to the City's challenges by encouraging "zero tolerance" street enforcement that prioritized officers making large numbers of stops, searches, and arrests—and often resorting to force—with minimal training and insufficient oversight from supervisors or through other accountability structures. These practices led to repeated violations of the constitutional and statutory rights, further eroding the community's trust in the police.

Proactive policing does not have to lead to these consequences. On the contrary, constitutional, community-oriented policing is proactive policing, but it is fundamentally different from the tactics employed in Baltimore for many years. Community policing depends on building relationships with all of the communities that a police department serves, and then jointly solving problems to ensure public safety. We encourage BPD to be proactive, to get to know Baltimore's communities more deeply, build trust, and reduce crime together with the communities it serves.

Fortunately, the current leadership of the City and the BPD already have taken laudable steps to reverse this course, including by revising BPD's use of force policies, taking steps toward enhancing accountability and transparency throughout the Department by, for example, beginning to equip officers with body worn cameras, and taking steps toward improving and expanding its community outreach to better engage its officers with the community they serve. Still, significant challenges remain. . . .

The Department of Justice and the City have entered into an Agreement in Principle that identifies categories of reforms the parties agree must be taken to remedy the violations of the Constitution and federal law described in this report. Both the Justice Department and the City seek input from all communities in Baltimore on the reforms that should be included in a comprehensive, court-enforceable consent decree to be negotiated by the Justice Department and the City in the coming months, and then entered as a federal court order.

As we have seen in jurisdictions across America, it is possible for law enforcement agencies to enhance their effectiveness by promoting constitutional policing and restoring community partnerships. Strengthening community trust in BPD will not only increase the effectiveness of BPD's law enforcement efforts, it will advance officer and public safety in a manner that serves the entire Baltimore community. Together with City officials and the people of Baltimore, we will work to make this a reality.

Source: U.S. Department of Justice, Civil Rights Division, *Investigation of the Baltimore City Police Department*, August 10, 2016, https://www.justice.gov/crt/file/883296/download.

Attorney General Loretta Lynch Responds to Dallas Police Shootings

In July 2016, a sniper shot and killed five police officers during a Black Lives Matter protest in Dallas, Texas. Although the gunman was not associated with Black Lives Matter, the intentional targeting of police officers generated intense criticism of movement. In her official statement on the shootings, Attorney General Loretta Lynch expresses sympathy for the fallen officers and their loved ones, but she also defends the protesters' right to be heard.

Good morning, and thank you all for being here.

Last night, at least five police officers were shot and killed, and several more were injured—along with two civilians—as they sought to protect a peaceful protest in Dallas, Texas. Our thoughts and condolences go out to the families who have lost loved ones. The Department of Justice—including the FBI, ATF, U.S. Marshals Service and U.S. Attorney's Office—is working closely with our state and local counterparts, and we intend to provide any assistance we can to investigate this attack, and to heal a community that has been severely shaken and deeply scarred by an unfathomable tragedy. This is an unfolding situation and we will provide additional information when it is available and appropriate.

This has been a week of profound grief and heartbreaking loss. The peaceful protest that was planned in Dallas last night was organized in response to the tragic deaths of Alton Sterling in Louisiana and Philando Castile in Minnesota. We have opened a civil rights investigation in Louisiana and we are providing assistance to local authorities in Minnesota who are leading the investigation there. Today, we are feeling the devastating loss of Dallas Area Rapid Transit Officer Brent Thompson and four other fallen officers whose names remain unreleased as we await notification of all the families. After the events of this week, Americans across the county are feeling a sense of helplessness, of uncertainty and of fear. These feelings are understandable and they are justified. But the answer must not be violence. The answer is never violence.

Rather, the answer must be action: calm, peaceful, collaborative and determined action. We must continue working to build trust between communities and law enforcement. We must continue working to guarantee every person in this country equal justice under the law. We must take a hard look at the ease with which wrongdoers can get their hands on deadly weapons and the frequency with which they use them. We must reflect on the kind of country we want to build and the kind of society we want to pass on to our children. We must reject the easy impulses of bitterness and rancor and embrace the difficult work of finding a path forward together. Above all, we must remind ourselves that we are all Americans—and that, as Americans, we share not just a common land, but a common life. Those we have lost this week have come from different neighborhoods and backgrounds—but today, they are mourned by officers and residents, by family and friends—by men and women and children who loved them, who needed them and who will miss them always. They are mourned by all of us.

To the families of all who lost their lives in this series of tragedies, we share your pain and your loss. To our brothers and sisters who wear the badge: I want you to know that I am deeply grateful for the difficult and dangerous work you do every day to keep our streets safe and our nations secure. I am heartbroken at this loss. And the Department of Justice will do all we can to support you in the days ahead. To those who seek to improve our country through peaceful protest and protected speech: I want you to know that your voice is important. Do not be discouraged by those who use your lawful actions as cover for their heinous violence. We will continue to safeguard your constitutional rights and to work with you in the difficult mission of building a better nation and a brighter future. And to all Americans: I ask you not to allow the events of this week to precipitate a "new normal" in our country. I ask you to turn to each other, not against each other as we move forward. Let us support one another. Let us help heal one another. And I urge you to remember, today and every day, that we are one nation. We are one people. And we stand together. May God bless the families and loved ones of all who were taken from us this week and comfort their grief with his everlasting grace. And may God bless the United States of America.

Source: U.S. Department of Justice, "Attorney General Loretta E. Lynch Delivers Statement on Dallas Shooting," Washington, DC, July 8, 2016, https://www.justice.gov/opa/speech/attorney-general-loretta-e-lynch-delivers-statement-dallas-shooting.

President Barack Obama Calls for Constructive Dialogue

At a press conference held three days after the Dallas police shootings, a reporter asked President Barack Obama to comment on the tactics employed by Black Lives Matters protesters. In his response, Obama encourages the protesters to be peaceful, respectful, and constructive in order to build public support for police reform. Such remarks met with criticism from some BLM activists, who felt the first black president did not do enough to advance their cause.

Michael A. Memoli, *Los Angeles Times*. You've commented in the past on some of the tactics of the Black Lives Matter movement that you suggested have been counterproductive. We've seen continued protests . . . overnight in many American cities over the Dallas tragedy. And as you prepare yourself to travel to Dallas, how would you advise the Black Lives Matter activists to approach this very sensitive issue—situation?

President Barack Obama. One of the great things about America is that individual citizens and groups of citizens can petition their government, can protest, can speak truth to power. And that is sometimes messy and controversial. But because of that ability to protest and engage in free speech, America, over time, has gotten better. We've all benefited from that.

The abolition movement was contentious. The effort for women to get the right to vote was contentious and messy. There were times when activists might have engaged in rhetoric that was overheated and occasionally counterproductive. But the point was to raise issues so that we, as a society, could grapple with it. The same was true with the civil rights movement and the union movement and the environmental movement, the antiwar movement during Vietnam. And I think what you're seeing now is part of that longstanding tradition.

What I would say is this: that whenever those of us who are concerned about fairness in the criminal justice system attack police officers, you are doing a disservice to the cause. First of all, any violence directed at police officers is a reprehensible crime, and it needs to be prosecuted. But even rhetorically, if we paint police in broad brush, without recognizing that the vast majority of police officers are doing a really good job and are trying to protect people and do so fairly and without racial bias, if our rhetoric does not recognize that, then we're going to lose allies in the reform cause.

Now, in a movement like Black Lives Matter, there's always going to be some folks who say things that are stupid or imprudent or overgeneralize or are harsh. And I don't think that you can hold well-meaning activists who are doing the right thing and peacefully protesting responsible for everything that is uttered at a protest site. But I would just say to everybody who's concerned about the issue of police shootings or racial bias in the criminal justice system that maintaining a truthful and serious and respectful tone is going to help mobilize American society to bring about real change. And that is our ultimate objective.

Now, this week, people felt hurt and angry, and so some of this is just venting. But I think that the overwhelming majority of people who are involved in the Black Lives Matter movement, what they really want to see is a better relationship between the police and the community so that they can feel that it's serving them. And the best way to do that is to bring allies aboard. That means—that includes, by the way, police departments that are doing the right thing, like Dallas, which has implemented the very reforms that Black Lives Matter is seeking. That's part of why it's so tragic that those officers were targeted in Dallas, a place that—because of its transparency and training and openness and engagement with the community—has drastically brought down the number of police shootings and complaints about misconduct.

The flip side of that—and this is the last point I'll make—is just as my hope would be that everybody who is involved in the Black Lives Matter movement or other civil rights organizations or who are protesting, just as I want all of them to maintain a respectful, thoughtful tone, because as a practical matter, that's what's going to get change done, I would hope that police organizations are also respectful of the frustrations that people in these communities feel and not just dismiss these protests and these complaints as political correctness or as politics or attacks on police. There are legitimate issues that have been raised, and there's data and evidence to back up the concerns that are being expressed by these protesters.

And if police organizations and departments acknowledge that there's a problem and there's an issue, then that, too, is going to contribute to real solutions. And as I said yesterday, that is what's going to ultimately help make the job of being a cop a lot safer. It is in the interest of police officers that their communities trust them and that the kind of rancor and suspicion that exists right now is alleviated.

So I'd like all sides to listen to each other. And that's what we'll hopefully be able to accomplish over the course of the next week and over the course of the remaining months that I'm President.

Source: Barack Obama, "Remarks Following a Meeting with Prime Minister Mariano Rajoy Brey of Spain and an Exchange with Reporters," Madrid, Spain, July 10, 2016, U.S. Government Printing Office, https://www.gpo.gov/fdsys/pkg/DCPD-201600459/html/DCPD-201600459.htm.

President Donald Trump Vows to Protect Police

In a speech delivered in May 2017 at a ceremony honoring law enforcement officers killed in the line of duty, President Donald Trump denounces Black Lives Matter protests for creating a hostile atmosphere that endangers police. He promises to end antipolice violence and usher in a new era of respect toward law enforcement.

We are gathered here today at the U.S. Capitol to pay tribute to those brave law enforcement officers who gave their lives in the line of duty. On this Peace Officers' Memorial Day, we thank God for having blessed so many of us with such incredible heroes—and we pledge our solidarity with their families and loved ones. . . .

Your presence here reminds us all of what is at stake on this sacred day of remembrance. Each May, during Police Week, new names of fallen police officers are added to the National Law Enforcement Memorial. This year, 394 brave souls join the over 20,000 men and women who gave up their lives in the line of duty to protect us. . . .

As you all know much too well, we are living through an era in which our police have been subject to unfair defamation and vilification, and, even worse—really, I mean, you see what's going on, you see what's going on—even worse, hostility and violence. More officers were slain last year in ambushes than in any year in more than two decades, including—and that's so incredible to even have to be speaking about this—the beloved officers killed in Baton Rouge, Louisiana, in yet another murderous attack on law enforcement. And we have some of those incredible families and survivors with us. . . .

The attacks on our police are a stain on the very fabric of our society, and you are entitled to leadership at the highest level that will draw a bright line in the sand—not a red line in the sand that isn't gone over—but a bright line in the sand. And we will protect you. That I can tell you. And we will say, "Enough is enough." The attacks on our police must end, and they must end right now. . . .

We must also end the reckless words of incitement that give rise to danger and give rise to violence. It is time to work with our cops, not against them, but to support them in making our streets safe; not to obstruct them—which we're doing, we obstruct them.

It is time for all Americans, from all parties and beliefs, to join together in a simple goal to ensure that every child in America has the right to grow up in safety, security and peace. True social justice means a future where every child, in every neighborhood, can play outside without fear, can walk home safely from school, and can live out the beautiful dreams that fill their heart. . . .

Freedom includes the right to be free—and I mean totally free—from crime and from violence. MS-13 [a Latino criminal gang] is going to be gone from our streets very soon, believe me.

When policing is reduced, it's often the poorest and most vulnerable Americans who are the first to suffer. We have all seen the tragic rise in violence and crimes in many of our disadvantaged communities. We've seen the unbearable horror of the shortcomings in Baltimore and Chicago that have cut short so many lives and so many beautiful, beautiful dreams.

We cannot stand for such violence. We cannot tolerate such pain. We cannot, under any circumstances, any longer turn a blind eye to this suffering that's going on any longer. And we won't. . . .

To everyone in the audience here today, I want you to know that my administration is determined—totally determined—to restore law and order and justice for all Americans, and we're going to do it quickly. . . .

America as a nation must always have the clarity to know the difference between good and evil, between right and wrong, and between those who uphold our laws and those who so easily break them. We owe it to the fallen to act according to our best and highest ideals. We owe it to their memory to put truth before politics, justice before agendas, and to put the safety and security of the American people above everything else. And we owe it to them to build a better future for all of America's wonderful children.

May today be the beginning of a new era of respect and appreciation for law enforcement. May this ceremony bring new hope to those in search of healing, harmony and peace. May Americans learn from the example of the heroes we have lost, and always remember to trust each other, work with each other, and love each other.

And finally, and so importantly, may God bless you. May God bless our police. And may God bless the United States of America. Thank you.

Source: Donald Trump, "Remarks by President Trump at the 36th Annual National Peace Officers' Memorial Service," May 15, 2017, https://www.c-span.org/video/?428451-1/president-calls-police-the-thin-blue-line-civilization-chaos.

FBI Report Warns of "Black Identity Extremists"

In August 2017, the FBI's Counterterrorism Division released an intelligence report that classified "black identity extremists" (BIEs) as a domestic terror threat. The report warned that BIEs appeared motivated to engage in violent attacks against law enforcement officers in response to perceived racism in American society. Leaders of the Black Lives Matter movement expressed concern that the report could lead to government surveillance and targeting of African Americans based on their political speech or activism.

Executive Summary

The FBI assesses it is very likely Black Identity Extremist[a] (BIE) perceptions of police brutality against African Americans spurred an increase in premeditated, retaliatory lethal violence against law

---

[a]The FBI defines black identity extremists as individuals who seek, wholly or in part, through unlawful acts of force or violence, in response to perceived racism and injustice in American society and some do so in furtherance of establishing a separate black homeland or autonomous black social institutions, communities, or governing organizations within the United States. This desire for physical or psychological separation is typically based on either a religious or political belief system, which is sometimes formed around or includes a belief in racial superiority or supremacy. The mere advocacy of political or social positions, political activism, use of strong rhetoric, or generalized philosophic embrace of violent tactics may not constitute extremism, and may be constitutionally protected.

enforcement and will very likely serve as justification for such violence. The FBI assesses it is very likely this increase began following the 9 August 2014 shooting of Michael Brown in Ferguson, Missouri, and the subsequent Grand Jury November 2014 declination to indict the police officers involved. The FBI assesses it is very likely incidents of alleged police abuse against African Americans since then have continued to feed the resurgence in ideologically motivated, violent criminal activity within the BIE movement. The FBI assesses it is very likely some BIEs are influenced by a mix of anti-authoritarian, Moorish sovereign citizen[b] ideology, and BIE ideology. The FBI has high confidence in these assessments, based on a history of violent incidents attributed to individuals who acted on behalf of their ideological beliefs, documented in FBI investigations and other law enforcement and open source reporting. The FBI makes this judgment with the key assumption the recent incidents are ideologically motivated.

Scope Note

This intelligence assessment focuses on individuals with BIE ideological motivations who have committed targeted, premeditated attacks against law enforcement officers since 2014. This assessment does not address BIEs who have attacked law enforcement officers during the course of officers' routine duties, such as responding to calls and traffic stops, in which violent actions were reactionary in nature.

This assessment addresses the following key intelligence questions:

- To what extent are BIEs' targeting interests retaliatory?
- What cross-programmatic relationships influence the BIE movement?

This assessment is the first FBI analytic intelligence product to assess influences between the sovereign citizen extremist movement and the black identity extremist movement. The FBI has previously

---

[b]The FBI defines sovereign citizen extremists as individuals who openly reject their U.S. citizenship status, believe that most forms of established government, authority, and institutions are illegitimate, and seek, wholly or in part, through unlawful acts of force or violence, to further their claim to be immune from government authority. The mere advocacy of political or social positions, political activism, use of strong rhetoric, or generalized philosophic embrace of violent tactics may not constitute extremism, and may be constitutionally protected.

reported on BIE retaliatory violence against law enforcement in two products, both of which had findings consistent with this assessment. The 23 March 2016 FBI intelligence bulletin, titled "Black Separatist Extremists' Call for Retaliation in Response to Police-Involved Incidents Could Incite Acts of Violence against Law Enforcement," assessed incidents involving allegations of law enforcement abuse and related legal proceedings would likely lead to BSE calls for violent retaliation and incite these domestic extremists to commit violent acts against law enforcement. The 14 November 2014 FBI intelligence bulletin, titled "Potential Criminal Reactions to Missouri Grand Jury Announcement," assessed the announcement of the grand jury's decision in the shooting death of Michael Brown in Ferguson would likely be exploited by some individuals to justify threats and attacks against law enforcement and critical infrastructure.

Suspects' Grievances Very Likely Lead to Violent Targeting of Law Enforcement

The FBI judges it is very likely BIE perceptions of police brutality against African Americans have become organizing drivers for the BIE movement since 2014, resulting in a spike of BIEs intentionally targeting law enforcement with violence. In all six targeted attacks since 2014, the FBI assesses it is very likely the BIE suspects acted in retaliation for perceived past police brutality incidents. Even though five of these attacks occurred following controversial police shootings of African Americans by white police officers, BIE targeting of officers was not, in every incident, based on their specific race. . . . [Details of the six incidents follow]

Perspective

BIEs have historically justified and perpetrated violence against law enforcement, which they perceived as representative of the institutionalized oppression of African Americans, but had not targeted law enforcement with premeditated violence for the nearly two decades leading up to the lethal incidents observed beginning in 2014. BIE violence peaked in the 1960s and 1970s in response to changing socioeconomic attitudes and treatment of blacks during the Civil Rights Movement. BIE groups, such as the Black Liberation Army (BLA), which was created in the early 1970s to "take up arms for the liberation and self-determination of black people in the United States," engaged in murders, bank robberies, kidnappings, racketeering, possession of explosives, and weapons smuggling.

- From 1970 to 1984, the BLA was involved in at least 38 criminal incidents, including 26 armed assaults, 3 assassinations, 4 bombings, and 4 hijackings and hostage takings. Almost half of these attacks took place in predominantly African American neighborhoods and targeted law enforcement officers without regard to their race according to an open source database.

BIE violence has been rare over the past 20 years and there is sparse evidence of any convergence with SCEs who adhere to Moorish beliefs, who have historically engaged in nonviolent fraudulent schemes—including production of fraudulent personal identification documents such as International Motorist Certifications, passports, vehicle titles and registrations, and birth certificates—in support of their claims of sovereignty. In addition, although non-Moorish SCEs have committed lethal violence against law enforcement in the past, this violence has typically occurred in response to encounters with law enforcement—for example, during traffic stops or the issuing of warrants—rather than through premeditated, targeted aggression. In addition, not all self-identified Moors are sovereign citizens, and not all sovereign citizen Moors engage in violence against law enforcement or other illegal activity.

The FBI has previously reported on BIE retaliatory violence against law enforcement in two products. This intelligence assessment addresses actual incidents of lethal retaliatory violence. The previous black identity extremism intelligence products discussed calls for potential retaliatory violence, not actual violent incidents. Recent lethal violent incidents may be indicative of a resurgence of targeted violence within the BIE movement.

Analysis of Alternatives

The FBI considered the alternative hypothesis that retaliatory violence against law enforcement is not ideologically motivated, but rather a result that some individuals may simply harbor animosity toward police and exploit racial tensions as an excuse to commit acts of violence. The FBI, however, assesses this alternative is very unlikely in the cases analyzed in this assessment because strictly criminal subjects typically commit spontaneous, "defensive" acts of violence against police rather than proactive targeting, and use idiosyncratic reasons unrelated to ideology, such as financial gain and personal disputes, to justify their actions. The FBI further judges it is very likely BIEs proactively target police and openly identify and justify their actions with social-political agendas commensurate with their perceived injustices against African Americans, and in some cases, their identified affiliations with violent extremist groups.

Outlook

The FBI assesses it is very likely that BIEs' perceptions of unjust treatment of African Americans and the perceived unchallenged illegitimate actions of law enforcement will inspire premeditated attacks against law enforcement over the next year. This may also lead to an increase in BIE group memberships, collaboration among BIE groups, or the appearance of additional violent lone offenders motivated by BIE rhetoric. The FBI further assesses it is very likely additional controversial police shootings of African Americans and the associated legal proceedings will continue to serve as drivers for violence against law enforcement. The FBI assesses it is likely police officers of minority groups are also targeted by BIEs because they are also representative of a perceived oppressive law enforcement system.

Possible indicators for BIEs posing a violent threat to law enforcement include advocating for violence against law enforcement, violent anti-white rhetoric, attempts to acquire illegal weapons or explosives, and affiliations with others in both the BSE and sovereign citizen extremist movements.

Source: Federal Bureau of Investigation, "Black Identity Extremists Likely Motivated to Target Law Enforcement Officers," *Intelligence Assessment*, August 3, 2017, https://assets.documentcloud.org/documents/4067711/BIE-Redacted.pdf.

Annotated Bibliography

Books

Patrisse Khan-Cullors and Asha Bandele, *When They Call You a Terrorist: A Black Lives Matter Memoir* (New York: St. Martin's Press, 2018).
   In this powerful best-selling memoir, Black Lives Matter (BLM) cofounder Khan-Cullors recalls the challenges of growing up black and queer in Los Angeles and describes how those experiences shaped her activism.

Christopher J. Lebron, *The Making of Black Lives Matter: A Brief History of an Idea* (New York: Oxford University Press, 2017).
   Lebron, a Yale University political philosopher, provides an intellectual history of the ideas about human respect and dignity that have influenced the BLM movement.

Wesley Lowery, *"They Can't Kill Us All": Ferguson, Baltimore, and a New Era in America's Racial Justice Movement* (New York: Little, Brown, 2016).
   Lowery, a journalist who covered the Ferguson protests on the ground for the *Washington Post*, offers an in-depth, first-person account of the birth of the BLM movement.

Keeanga-Yamahtta Taylor, *From #BlackLivesMatter to Black Liberation* (Chicago: Haymarket Books, 2016).
   This book by a Princeton University professor of African American Studies analyzes the BLM movement within the broader historical context of the black struggle for liberation.

Periodicals

"Black Lives Matter Everywhere" Series, *Conversation*, October 2017, https://theconversation.com/au/topics/black-lives-matter-everywhere-44608.
   In recognition of the cofounders of BLM being awarded the Sydney Peace Prize, the *Conversation* published a series of scholarly articles about the movement's impact around the world.

"Black Lives Matter: What We Must Do Now," *Essence* (special issue), January 2015, https://www.essence.com/2015/01/06/historic-essence-cover-and-path-forward.
   This special issue of the leading magazine for black women features essays on the message and impact of the BLM movement by female activists, leaders, and cultural figures.

Jelani Cobb, "The Matter of Black Lives," *New Yorker*, March 14, 2016, https://www.newyorker.com/magazine/2016/03/14/where-is-black-lives-matter-headed.
   Cobb traces the origins of the BLM movement through interviews with several of its leading figures and examines the future challenges for black activism post-Obama.

Elizabeth Day, "#BlackLivesMatter: The Birth of a New Civil Rights Movement," *Guardian*, July 19, 2015, https://www.theguardian.com/world/2015/jul/19/blacklivesmatter-birth-civil-rights-movement.
   This comprehensive article shows how key figures in the early days of BLM used social media tools to turn a moment into a movement.

Jay Caspian Kang, "Our Demand Is Simple: Stop Killing Us," *New York Times*, May 4, 2015, https://www.nytimes.com/2015/05/10/magazine/our-demand-is-simple-stop-killing-us.html.
   In this in-depth profile of Ferguson protesters DeRay Mckesson and Johnetta Elzie, Kang explores how online activism helped spark a national conversation about police violence.

Touré, "A Year Inside the Black Lives Matter Movement," *Rolling Stone*, December 7, 2017, https://www.rollingstone.com/politics/news/toure-inside-black-lives-matter-w513190.
   Touré reflects on the challenges facing BLM following the election of Donald Trump and the white supremacist rally in Charlottesville, Virginia.

Websites

Black Lives Matter, https://blacklivesmatter.com/.
   The official site of BLM offers a wealth of information about the movement's founders, guiding principles, chapters, emerging issues, upcoming actions, and ways to get involved.

Black Lives Matter Syllabus, http://www.blacklivesmattersyllabus.com/.
    Created by New York University (NYU) professor Frank Leon Roberts, the
Black Lives Matter Syllabus is an online, public educational curriculum that pro-
vides access to a wide variety of resources for teaching and learning about the
BLM movement, police violence, and institutional racism.

Campaign Zero, https://www.joincampaignzero.org/#vision.
    Created by BLM activists, this website outlines a 10-point plan of action for ending
police violence, including body cameras, sensitivity training, community oversight, and
demilitarization.

Deen Freelon, Charlton D. McIlwain, and Meredith D. Clark, "Beyond the Hashtags:
    #Ferguson, #BlackLivesMatter, and the Online Struggle for Offline Justice,"
    Center for Media and Social Impact, February 2016, http://cmsimpact.org/wp
    -content/uploads/2016/03/beyond_the_hashtags_2016.pdf.
    This comprehensive research report examines the growth of the BLM movement
through the lens of activists' uses of online media in 2014 and 2015.

Mapping Police Violence, https://mappingpoliceviolence.org/.
    This website created by BLM activists provides detailed information about all the
people killed by police in the United States since 2015, including statistics, reports,
trends, city comparisons, and an interactive map.

Index

About the Author

LAURIE COLLIER HILLSTROM is a freelance writer and editor based in Brighton, Michigan. She is the author of more than 40 books in the areas of American history, biography, and current events. Some of her previously published works include *Defining Moments: The Underground Railroad*, *Defining Moments: Plessy v. Ferguson*, and *Defining Moments: Jackie Robinson and the Integration of Baseball.*